The Jury: Its Role in American Society

The Jury: Its Role in American Society

Rita J. Simon
University of Illinois

LexingtonBooks
D.C. Heath and Company
Lexington, Massachusetts
Toronto

Library of Congress Cataloging in Publication Data

Simon, Rita James.
The jury.

Includes index.
1. Jury—United States. I. Title.
KF8972.S55 347'.73'75 77-17682
ISBN 0-669-02086-9

Published simultaneously in Canada.

Printed in the United States of America.

International Standard Book Number: 0-669-02086-9

Library of Congress Catalog Card Number: 77-17682

For
Julian, David, Judith, and Daniel

Contents

	List of Figures	ix
	List of Tables	xi
	Preface	xiii
Part I	*Images of the Jury: Past and Present*	1
Chapter 1	**Introduction and Brief History of the American Jury**	3
Chapter 2	**The View of the Jury in American Literature, the Press, and the Bench**	11
	A View from Selections in American Literature and Theater	11
	A View from the Mass Media Magazines	14
	A View from the Judiciary	20
Part II	*Research on the Jury: Empirical Examination of How the Jury Functions*	27
Chapter 3	**The Influence of Demographic and Social Characteristics on Juror Selection and Performance**	29
	Representativeness	29
	Jury Selection	31
	Jurors' Social Characteristics and Verdicts	38
	Participation and Influence within the Jury	41
	Concluding Remarks	45
Chapter 4	**The Rationality of Jury Deliberations and Verdicts**	49
	Experimental Juries	52
	Jury Treatment of the Rules of Law	52
	Expert Testimony	57
	How Consensus Is Reached in the Juryroom	63
	Concluding Remarks	69
Chapter 5	**Jury Size and Decision Rule** *David A. Vollrath* and *James H. Davis*	73
	Jury Size	74

	Jury Decision Rule	77
	Interaction of Size and Decision Rule	78
	Conceptual Issues	79
	"Thought Experiments"	85
	Discussion: Thought Experiments on Size and Decision Rule	97
	Summary and Conclusions	100
Part III	*The Jury in the Limelight: How Independent and Impartial Is It?*	107
Chapter 6	**The Impact of Pretrial Publicity on the Jury**	109
	Influence of the Mass Media on Public Attitudes and Opinion	110
	Studies that Bear Directly on the Fair Trial/Free Press Controversy	111
	Studies Based on Simulated Exposure to Pretrial Publicity	111
	A Study Based on Exposure to Actual Pretrial Publicity	115
	Concluding Remarks	117
Chapter 7	**The American Jury: Instrument of Justice or of Prejudice and Conformity?**	123
	Political Trials in the Late 1940s and Early 1950s	124
	Political Trials in the Late 1960s and Early 1970s	131
	Political Trials of the Mid-1970s	142
	Concluding Remarks	145
	Index	153
	About the Author	159

List of Figures

4-1	Average Participation per Member of a Coalition, Sizes One to Six (Minority Coalitions Only)	67
5-1	Probability of a Jury Conviction (P_G) as a Function of Individual Guilt Performances (P_G) for Several Different Group Sizes (r)	87
5-2	Probability of Conviction, Acquittal, and Hung Jury	90
5-3	Probability of Each Verdict Alternative	92
5-4	Probability of a Conviction (P_G) in Twelve-Person Juries as a Function of Individual Preferences for Guilt (P_G)	94
5-5	Individual Juror Preference Distributions	95

List of Tables

3–1	Percentage Rates of Participation in Civil Jury Deliberations by Occupation and Sex of Juror	42
3–2	Average Votes Received as Helpful Jurors by Occupation and Sex	43
3–3	Percentage Rates of Participation in Criminal and Civil Jury Deliberations by Occupation	44
3–4	Choice of Foreman according to Occupation	45
4–1	Percent of Judge and Jury Agreement and Disagreement in Criminal Cases	50
4–2	Percent of Judge and Jury Agreement on Liability in Personal Injury Cases	50
4–3	Percent of Disagreement between Judges and Juries by Complexity and Closeness of Evidence	51
4–4	Probability of Guilt by the Beyond-a-Reasonable-Doubt Standard	56
4–5	Probability of Negligence by the Preponderance-of-Evidence Standard	56
4–6	Commitment Information by Jury Verdicts	61
4–7	Jurors' Expectations about the Court's Disposition of the Defendant by Commitment Instruction	62
4–8	Relationship between Individual and Group Decisions	64
4–9	First Ballot Votes by Jury Verdicts	65
5–1	Matrices Illustrating Social-Decision-Rule Possibilities for Criminal Juries of Six, Nine, and Twelve Persons	81
5–2	Examples of Possible Social-Decision-Scheme Matrices for Criminal Juries of Six, Nine, and Twelve Persons	83
6–1	Verdict Distribution before the Trial by Sensational and Conservative Newspaper Reports	113
6–2	Verdict Distribution after the Trial by Sensational and Conservative Newspaper Reports	114
6–3	Final Verdicts and Votes of Mineola Juries	115

6-4	Final Verdicts and Votes of Brooklyn Jurors	116
7-1	Summary of Important Political Trials from 1945 to Mid-1970s	124

Preface

I started doing research on the American jury in 1954 when I began my studies for the doctorate in sociology at the University of Chicago. In the 1950s the jury was under attack as an outmoded institution that needed replacement. Shortly before, in Great Britain, the jury had been retained for criminal trials, but was no longer used for civil actions. A movement led and supported by members of the appellate bench urged the United States to follow the British example. The initial research output of the Chicago Jury Project was examined with an eye for evidence supporting the arguments of those who favored doing away with the jury, at least in civil actions. But detractors of the jury found little in the early publications to strengthen their arguments. As time passed and the major work of the project appeared in print (*The American Jury* by Harry Kalven and Hans Zeisel, and my volume, *The Jury and the Defense of Insanity*), it became clear that the jury had passed empirical examination with high marks. Most of the subsequent research on the jury conducted by legal scholars and social scientists in the 1960s and 1970s supports the findings of the Chicago project. The jury also has been praised by the media for its role in the major political trials of the late 1960s and early 1970s.

Today, a quarter of a century later, the jury seems to be enjoying more popularity and respect than it has at any time since at least the turn of the century, and perhaps since before the Civil War.

Part I
Images of the Jury: Past and Present

1 Introduction and Brief History of the American Jury

Research on the jury has been in vogue since 1953 when the Law School of the University of Chicago initiated a major program in law and the behavioral sciences and decided the American jury system would be one of its areas of inquiry.[1] That inquiry resulted in almost one hundred articles and two monographs about many aspects of jury behavior including jury competence, representativeness, motivation, the social-psychological dynamics of jury deliberations, and perceptions of the jury's performance by trial court judges. In retrospect, however, it is apparent that although the work done at Chicago told us a great deal about the American jury system, it did not provide answers to all of the questions about the jury and it even raised some new ones. Much of the research on the jury that has been done since the Chicago project has evolved from the research conducted there.

In the past quarter of a century, the jury has not only enjoyed popularity as a topic for research but it has also been called into service more frequently during this period than in the preceding two and a half decades. Johnson has argued that "over the last half-century, the jury's place in the American adjudicative process has been enormously diminished."[2] Quoting from Chambliss and Seidman Johnson reported that "today less than two percent of all cases are so [jury] decided. "The jury," he continued, "retains mostly a symbolic significance." Johnson concluded that "the core of the twentieth century story is the destruction of the jury."[3] But the data contained in the December 13, 1973 issue of *U.S. News and World Report* belie that contention. *U.S. News* reported that in 1973 two million citizens were called for jury duty and 150,000 jury trials were held in federal, state, and local courts combined. In federal district courts alone there were 9,251 jury trials. *U.S. News and World Report* claimed that the 1973 figures represented a 57 percent increase in jury trials over the past decade.[4]

In 1955 Kalven and Zeisel estimated that there were 2,290 jury trials in federal district courts and 53,380 jury trials in state courts throughout the United States.[5] If one considers the differences between 1955 and 1973, there has been almost two and a half times as many jury trials in 1973 than in 1955. In the federal district courts there has been over three times as many. These figures attest dramatically to the fact that the jury system is neither a dying, nor a symbolic institution. On the contrary, its usage has increased considerably in the last two decades.

My purpose in writing this book is to organize, edit, and comment upon much of the major research that has been done on the American jury from the

1950s to the present. In carrying out this task, I have focused on the following issues: How representative is the jury of the community from which it has been selected? How important are the jurors' demographic and socioeconomic characteristics in the decision process? How motivated is the jury to carry out the tasks assigned to it? How does the jury go about reaching its verdict? How well does the jury understand the testimony of expert witnesses and the instructions it receives from the judge? To what extent does the jury's verdict reflect the evidence presented and the rules of law it was told to apply? Does the size of the jury influence the length of time it takes to reach its decision and the type of decision it reaches? Does the verdict form (unanimous versus 9 to 3 or majority) affect the type of decision the jury makes? How satisfied are judges and jurors with the jury's performance? Are jurors' verdicts prejudiced by pretrial publicity? How effective has the jury been in maintaining its independence from both the judiciary and the community, especially in controversial political trials?

The topics just mentioned provide a quick summary of the range and diversity of issues that have been studied. A few comments about the varieties of methods and research designs that have been applied to the study of the jury also seem appropriate. In the Chicago studies, the jury was studied experimentally by having real jurors under the jurisdiction of the court listen to recorded trials based on real transcripts. The deliberations were also recorded. Demographic information about the jurors' socioeconomic status, religious and ethnic characteristics, prior experience with jury service, and attitudes toward law related issues were obtained from questionnaires that jurors filled out before and after the trial.

Another approach involved interviewing jurors after the trial was over and they had completed their deliberations. Each juror was asked to describe the trial as he or she saw it and to report what happened during the deliberations. From interviews with each of the members of the jury, the deliberations could then be reconstructed. The tensions, conflicts, and consensus process would be described from twelve individual perspectives.

A third approach involved contacting trial court judges in different parts of the country and arranging with them to report on all of the trials they heard for a stipulated time period that involved a jury. The judge provided a brief summary of the facts in the cases, the length and complexity of the trial, the charges, the defendant's characteristics, the jury's verdict, and then commented on whether he agreed or disagreed with that verdict.

In the years that have passed since the Chicago project, research on the jury has relied upon students to perform as jurors under laboratory-like conditions. Role players have been inserted into mock jury deliberations and variations in the size and verdict forms of experimental juries have been manipulated. Many of the findings that have emerged from these studies will be reported in this volume. But the emphasis will be primarily on the substantive findings as they bear upon the issues cited above rather than on the elegance, imaginativeness, or adequacy of the research designs.

Before turning to those studies, a brief history of the American jury is included. It is followed by a chapter describing how the jury has been perceived by the American press, by writers of American fiction, and by members of the bench and bar.

In the last section, we return to an evaluation of the independence of the jury by reporting its willingness and capacity for putting aside pre-trial publicity and its effectiveness as a bulwark for democracy. The latter is done by examining how the jury has performed in the three decades following the end of World War II, when it sat on some of the most dramatic political trials ever held in this country.

Historians have traced the origins of the jury to 11th century England when it took the form of a group of the defendant's neighbors who were called in to answer questions from their own knowledge.[6] Thus, jurors served as both witnesses and triers of the facts. It was not until the end of the 15th century that jurors ceased to serve as witnesses and came to function exclusively as triers of the facts. According to Marshall, "by 1689 the jury in criminal cases, with its power to reject the Crown's accusation, had evolved to such a point that its preservation was one of the main purposes of the English Declaration and Bill of Rights."[7]

The jury system reached American shores in 1607 when James I granted a charter to the Virginia Company and the Company established the community of Jamestown. Petit juries in the Virginia colony were composed of twelve men but records show that some juries contained as many as thirteen, fourteen, and in one instance twenty-four.

> In general, felony trials were held in one day. When the case was given to the jury, it was locked up without food or water until it reached a verdict. A juryman could not leave his fellows until a verdict was reached, which, as one writer has noted, made prolonged disagreement practically unknown.[8]

During the colonial period the jury became a symbol of rebellion against the Crown and a bulwark in favor of democracy. The jury's performance in the trial of John Peter Zenger (1735) stands out because the New York jury found Zenger not guilty of libel on grounds that what he had written about the royal governor was true.

The first Congress of the American colonies, which met in October 1765, included trial by jury among its inventory of essential rights and liberties. The First Continental Congress (October 1774) declared:

> that the respective colonies are entitled to the common law of England, and more especially to the great and inestimable privilege of being tried by their peers of the vicinage, according to the course of that law.

The Declaration of Independence denounced the Crown's puppet judges and objected to the King "depriving us in many cases of the benefit of trial by jury."

The U.S. Constitution in Article III, Section 2, states:

> The Trial of all Crimes, except in Cases of Impeachment, shall be by jury; and such Trial shall be held in the State where the said Crimes shall have been committed.

The Sixth Amendment to the Constitution guarantees the right of trial by jury in the following passage:

> In all criminal prosecutions, the accused shall enjoy the right to a speedy and public trial by an impartial jury of the state and district wherein the crime shall have been committed.

Supreme Court decisions later interpreted the due process clause of the Fourteenth Amendment to apply to state prosecutions as well.

During his travels in the United States in the first decade of the 19th century, de Tocqueville compared American and English juries as follows:

> The institution of the jury may be aristocratic or democratic, according to the class from which the jurors are taken; it always preserves its republican character, in that it placed the real direction of society in the hands of the governed, or of a portion of the governed, and not in that of the government. . . .
>
> In England the jury is selected from the aristocratic portion of the nation, the aristocracy makes the laws, applies the laws, and punishes infractions of the laws; everything is established upon a consistent footing, and England may with truth be said to constitute an aristocratic republic. In the United States the same system is applied to the whole people. Every American citizen is both an eligible and a legally qualified voter. The jury system as it is understood in America appears to me to be as direct and as extreme a consequence of sovereignty of the people as universal suffrage. They are two instruments of equal power, which contribute to the supremacy of the majority. All the sovereigns who have chosen to govern by their own authority, and to direct society instead of obeying its directions, have destroyed or enfeebled the institution of the jury. The Tudor monarchs sent to prison jurors who refused to convict, and Napoleon caused them to be selected by his agents. . . .
>
> The jury contributed powerfully to form the judgment and to increase the natural intelligence of a people; and this, in my opinion, is its greatest advantage. It may be regarded as a gratuitous public school, ever open, in which every juror learns his rights, enters into daily communication with the most learned and enlightened members of the upper classes, and becomes practically acquainted with the laws, which

> are brought within the reach of his capacity by the efforts of the bar, the advice of the judge, and even the passions of the parties. I think that the practical intelligence and political good sense of the Americans are mainly attributable to the long use that they have made of the jury in civil causes.[9]

Tocqueville concluded:

> Thus, the jury, which is the most energetic means of making the people rule, is also the most efficacious means of teaching it how to rule well.[10]

In the sixty years that intervened between the ratification of the Constitution and the secession of the Southern states that led to the Civil War, the jury played an important role in the issues that resulted in the war. By and large Northern juries refused to convict persons who aided escaping slaves and thereby effectively nullified the Federal Fugitive Slave Law.

But if the jury's record is consistently on the side of personal liberty and justice on the fugitive slave issue and the personal liberty laws in the period prior to the Civil War, its record is marked by prejudice and violations of the spirit and form of the Constitution in the period following the Civil War, especially in the reconstructed Southern states. Juries in the South following the Civil War were composed primarily of ex-Confederates whose decisions in cases involving blacks accused of crimes, or whites accused of crimes against blacks, were consistently against blacks. By not overtly violating the Thirteenth, Fourteenth, and Fifteenth Amendments, the Southern states could continue for almost a century to deprive their black citizens of most of their civil rights including voting and jury service.

Early in the 20th century a popular theme of social-minded jurisprudence was that it was the jury's responsibility to nullify unjust laws. Roscoe Pound wrote:

> Jury lawlessness is the great corrective of law in its actual administration. The will of the state at large imposed on a reluctant community, the will of a majority imposed on a vigorous and determined minority, find the same obstacle in the local jury that formerly confronted kings and ministers.[11]

In *The American Jury,* Kalven and Zeisel called attention to the role that the jury performed during the 1920s when it consistently nullified prohibition laws.[12]

Kadish and Kadish commented on the jury's obligations vis-à-vis unjust cases as follows:

> In landmark cases, particularly involving criminal libel and sedition, the jury invoked its power to nullify what were widely regarded as unjust

> laws. These actions are commonly cited not as regrettable departures from the role of law, but as historic and seminal acts, like the Magna Carta and the Bill of Rights, by which men asserted their right to be free of unjust laws. . . .
>
> The duty of the jury is indeed to find the facts upon the basis of the evidence presented and to issue a general verdict by applying those facts to the propositions of law given by the judge. This is the rule and it imposes an obligation to comply. But it is not therefore an absolute and unyielding obligation. Sometimes the jury's common sense perceptions, considerations of fairness to the defendant, or appraisal of the law (in contrast to the judge's statement of it) are so weighty that they justify departure from the requirement that the jury defer to the judge's instructions. Some roles, that is, permit departures from the very rules that bind their agents when the agents are satisfied that there is not merely reason, but extreme good reason for doing so. They are capable of recognizing conflicts between role ends and the obligatory means regulating their achievement, and of making provision for resolving the conflict.[13]

The jury's response to politically controversial trials involving first amendment constitutional issues in the period following World War II is a major theme of part III.

Notes

1. This is not to say that there were no empirical studies of the jury prior to the Chicago project. For example, in 1924 Marston published the results of his experiment on how male and female jurors respond to testimony in William M. Marston, "Studies in Testimony," *Journal of Criminal Law and Criminology* 15 (1924): 5-31. In the 1930s law students at Cornell University served on mock juries. Those studies were reported in H.P. Weld and E.R. Danzig, "A Study of the Way in which a Verdict Is Reached by a Jury," *American Journal of Psychology* 53 (1940): 518-536, and H.P. Weld and M.F. Roff, "A Study in the Formation of Opinion Based Upon Legal Evidence," *American Journal of Psychology* 51 (1938): 609-628.

2. Bruce Johnson, "Inequality in the Courtroom: The Social Composition of Juries," unpublished manuscript (1976), p. 12.

3. Ibid., p. 15.

4. *U.S. News and World Report* (December 31, 1973): 28-30.

5. Harry Kalven, Jr., and Hans Zeisel, *The American Jury* (Boston: Little, Brown, 1966), p. 503.

6. For this section, I relied heavily on the essay by Harold M. Hyman and Catherine M. Tarrant, "Aspects of American Trial Jury History," in Rita J. Simon (ed.), *The Jury System in America* (Beverly Hills, Calif.: Sage Publications, 1975), pp. 23-44.

7. Rita J. Simon and Prentice Marshall, "The Jury System," in Stuart Nagel (ed.), *The Rights of the Accused* (Beverly Hills, Calif.: Sage Publications, 1972), pp. 211-233.

8. Hyman and Tarrant, *The Jury System in America,* p. 26.

9. Alex de Tocqueville, "Trial By Jury in the United States Considered as a Political Institution," in Phillips Bradley (ed.), *Democracy in America,* trans. by Henry Reeve, revised by Francis Bowen (New York: Alfred A. Knopf, Inc., 1966), pp. 291-297. Copyright © 1966 by Alfred A. Knopf, Inc. Reprinted with permission.

10. Ibid., p. 297.

11. Mortimer R. Kadish and Sanford H. Kadish, "The Institutionalization of Conflict," in J. Tapp and F. Levine (eds.), *Law, Justice and the Individual in Society: Psychological and Legal Issues* (New York: Holt, Rinehart and Winston, 1977), p. 311. Copyright © 1977 by Holt, Rinehart and Winston. Reprinted by permission of Holt, Rinehart and Winston.

12. Kalven and Zeisel, *The American Jury,* p. 296.

13. Ibid., p. 311.

2 The View of the Jury in American Literature, the Press, and the Bench

Much of the empirical research on the jury gives high marks to its performance and to the motivation of its participants. Whatever biases researchers may have held about the efficacy of the jury system, the intelligence of its participants, and the correctness of its decisions, the results they report are usually positive and supportive of the maintenance of the system. Yet a review of the image of the jury held by leading writers in American literature reveals a consistently negative, disparaging picture. In those passages, jurors seem to represent the collective prejudices and ignorance of the community. They are described as ill-willed, malevolent types who seek revenge and retribution even at the cost of justice.

Another forum in which the jury has received more negative than positive evaluations is at the hands of the bench, some of whom seem puzzled at the persistent inclusion of untrained amateurs into the complex technical world of the judiciary. They are puzzled not only by the fact that lay persons are allowed to participate in that world, but that they are given such important responsibilities as the weighing and sifting of evidence, and of reaching a decision that is binding upon the court and the parties involved. In recent years, there are signs that the negative assessment has changed, perhaps as a result of the publication of research findings that rather consistently demonstrate jury competence.

Still a third forum in which the behavior of the jury has been scrutinized is in the mass media magazines. Among these judges the verdicts are more mixed and evaluations tend to be made on the basis of how well the jury has performed in a particular case.

This chapter illustrates some of the ways in which the jury has been depicted by writers of American literature, members of the bench, and the mass media.

A View from Selections in American Literature and Theater

The jury room has not been a frequent setting, nor has the theme of how and what the jury does been a major topic in American literature.[1] When the jury has appeared in American fiction, however, it has not been characterized positively or admiringly. The most usual characterization of the jury is that it is incompetent and ill-motivated. Its deliberations often reveal ignorance, personal prejudice, and lack of concern. The jurors' presumed impartiality is often shown to have been compromised by local, family, racial, and/or political prejudice. It is also characterized as an institution in which its members are easily corruptible by money, fear, the enticement of a better job or a gain in status or power, and manipulation by skillful attorneys.

Watts locates the jury in the writings of James Fenimore Cooper, Mark Twain, Theodore Dreiser, Stephen Vincent Benet, John Barth, William Faulkner, Robert Penn Warren, Harper Lee, William Dickey, Ayn Rand, Elmer Rice, George Kaufman and Marc Connelly, Arthur Miller, and Stanley Elkins. While this list includes several of the major writers in American literature (Cooper, Twain, Dreiser, Faulkner), it does not contain the names of Nathaniel Hawthorne, Herman Melville, Henry James, and Ernest Hemingway, none of whom treated the jury in his work.

For James Fenimore Cooper, the jury represented mob or majority rule. In *The Ways of the Hour* (1850) Cooper described jury tampering on a massive scale. As Watts reports it:

> Lawyers for both the state and the defendant practice the art of "pillowing" or "horseshedding": lawyer's agents are hired to spread rumors throughout the general community both before and during the trial. Such rumors either directly or indirectly reach the ears of jurors who are, of course, members of the community before the trial and who, after they become jurors, enjoy social intercourse with nonjurors at the "horsesheds," which they have been allowed to visit during court recesses for the very practical purpose of checking on the feed and care of their horses. So significant is the work of these agents that jury selection often depends on just which agents have "gained the ear" of the prospective jurors. According to Cooper, the work of these paid agents is supplemented and even complemented by the journalists whose method of news gathering "threatens to set at defiance all laws, principles, and facts".[2]

Theodore Dreiser's treatment of the jury focused more on its incompetence than on its prejudice or its weakness of will. In *The Financier* he has Frank Cowperwood's lawyers characterize the jury as

> an ordinary body of men not trained in finance, were not capable mentally . . . of dealing with such a subtle problem. They could not possibly be made to understand the ramifications of finance. . . ., Such a case . . . should not be tried by a jury at all. It ought to be submitted to a committee of financial experts. . . .[3]

The jury is portrayed in another Dreiser novel, *The American Tragedy*. Here Dreiser focused on the intricate process of selecting the jury that would decide the fate of Clyde Griffith, the defendant, charged with the murder of his pregnant working class girl friend. Dreiser described the jury, that had taken five days to select, as follows:

> And such men—odd and grizzled, or tan and wrinkled, farmers and county storekeepers, with here and there a Ford agent, a keeper of an inn at Tom Dixon's Lake, a salesman in Hamburger's dry goods store at Bridgeburg, and a peripatetic insurance agent residing in Purday just north of Grass Lake. And with but one exception, all religious, if not moral, and all convinced of Clyde's guilt before they sat down, but still because of their almost unanimous conception of themselves as fair and open-minded men, and because they were so interested to sit as jurors in this exciting case, convinced that they could pass fairly and impartially on the facts presented to them.[4]

After the jury reached its verdict and found the defendant guilty of an act that he had in fact planned to commit, but did not carry out, Dreiser described how the jury finally reached consensus.

> Yet out of the whole twelve but one man—Samuel Upham, a druggist—politically opposed to Mason [the state's attorney] and taken with the personality of Jephson [one of Clyde's lawyers]—sympathizing with Belknap and Jephson. And so pretending that he had doubts as to the completeness of Mason's proof until at last after five ballots were taken he was threatened with exposure and the public rage and obloquy which was sure to follow in case the jury was hung. "We'll fix you. You won't get by with this without the public knowing exactly where you stand." Whereupon, having a satisfactory drug business in North Mansfield, he at once decided that it was best to pocket this opposition to Mason and agree.[5]

Racial prejudice on the part of the jury is dealt with explicitly in Harper Lee's *To Kill a Mockingbird* (1960) when a black man is found guilty and sentenced to death on circumstantial evidence. The jury is composed of white men from poor but respectable rural families. According to Watts:

> The townspeople who would, it is implied, have granted an acquittal do not serve on juries because as merchants they fear losing business and also because "serving on a jury forces a man to make up his mind and declare himself about something."[6]

In Robert Penn Warren's *World Enough and Time* (1950) the jury is depicted more positively than it is in most American literature. The defendant, Beaumont, was accused of murdering a prominent Kentucky political leader. In the story he maintained his innocence throughout the trial and fooled his own lawyer, but not the jury. According to Watts, "the jury's judgment represents the world's or the community's opinion, or the world's sense of truth."[7] Earlier in the novel, Warren had described the deliberation of a jury as follows:

> When the jury was hung, and the hour grown late when men go home to bed, a juror proposed that they should settle the question by a

> game of Old Sledge, for, as he said, "We don't know a gol-durned thing about this fellow, nohow." So the cards were fetched and the game commenced between the two champions of the opposed factions of the jury. On the stroke of midnight the score was seven to seven, when the hanging champion threw the jack and won the game. So the gallows was built and on it was nailed the Jack of Spades. When the man was brought forth on the appointed day and stood on his own coffin on the cart, he cursed them all soundly for the injustice that he, being a good man at the cards, had not been allowed to turn even one to save his neck.[8]

In another symbolic characterization of the jury, Stephen Vincent Benet assembled a group of sinners to serve as jurors in the trial of Jabez Stone. Stone, the defendant, had become a wealthy farmer and state senator in New Hampshire because he had mortgaged his soul to the Devil. When, after ten years, the mortgage fell due, Stone asked Daniel Webster to represent him against the Devil. In the subsequent trial, the jurors vote for acquittal because as one of them said:

> Perhaps 'tis not in strict accordance with the evidence . . . but even the damned may salute the eloquence of Mr. Webster.[9]

In essence, Benet had his jury of the damned ignore the law and render a merciful verdict.

In the theater, the jury has a role in Rice's *The Adding Machine* (1923), and in the dream sequence in Kaufman and Connelly's *Beggar on Horseback* (1924). In Ayn Rand's play, *The Night of January 16th* (1933), the jury is composed of volunteers from the audience who sit on the stage during the performance and announce their decision publicly. In the play the victim's mistress was charged with his murder. The final lines of the play depend on the jury's decision. According to Watts, "in the only tally kept of the decisions of the audience-jurors, the vote was three to two in favor of acquittal during the six-month run of the play on Broadway."[10]

In this brief examination of the jury's portrayal in American literature and theater, the jury is more often depicted negatively and cynically than it is in positive and admiring tones. The jury is more often described as representing the lowest common denominator of the people rather than as the common man personified by dignity, independence, and morality. The jury as an institution in American literature is generally tainted by prejudice, ignorance, and lack of will.

A View from the Mass Media Magazines

The following review of how the jury has been depicted in some of the leading weekly and monthly magazines from 1945 to 1975 does not pretend to be exhaustive. It does claim however to be representative of the opinion and perspectives that have appeared in those mass circulation periodicals over the thirty-year period.[11] Twenty-one articles were selected from the following sources: *Colliers, Harpers, Look, Life, Newsweek, New York Times Magazine, New Yorker, Reader's Digest, Saturday Evening Post, Time, U.S. News and World Report.* The titles offer a quick purview of the issues with which they have dealt. The following are samples: "Would a Lawyer Pick You as a Juror," "Something's Wrong With Our Jury System," "Jury Tampering in Tennessee," "Why People Complain About Jury Duty," "Verdict on Women Jurors," "Ear in the Jury Room." In almost all of the selections, the main theme was the jury's competence. Discussions of motivation, prejudice and representativeness were usually considered within the context of the competency issue.

An article in the *Reader's Digest,* "Would a Lawyer Pick You as a Juror," focused on the type of strategies and tricks lawyers have used to pick jurors who would be favorable to their cases.[12]

> [T]he lawyer's first care is to select jurors who look, sound—yes, and sometimes *smell*—favorable to his case. . . . One solid friend in the jury room may mean more than a week of forensic pleading.[13]

The article contained numerous anecdotes and examples of how lawyers using a well-honed intuition based on many years of courtroom experience can tell whether a certain type of juror would be favorably disposed to his case. For example, if the defendant was "under the influence" at the time the crime was committed, look for a juror with a red nose or try to get a close smell to see if any of the prospective jurors indulged in "morning eye-openers." To the defense counsel, Irishmen are always welcome on the jury because, in the words of Clarence Darrow, "his imagination will place him in the dock, where he will simultaneously be trying himself and thinking up reasons for letting himself off." On the other hand, defense lawyers are suspicious of pharmacists and accountants as the former are "always counting little pills," and the latter are too "ledgerminded." One can tell an intelligent juror by the Phi Beta Kappa key dangling from his watch chain, and such jurors are welcomed in civil suits involving complex legal or scientific technicalities. However, lawyers ordinarily steer away from "too brainy" jurors. One lawyer expressed his preference for jurors of "submedium intelligence" who can be ". . . led down irrelevant lanes of reasoning, and brought to tears by the liberal use of emotional onions." The article recounts how, during the trial, lawyers employ numerous subtle ploys to influence jurors. One lawyer wore an outlandish hand-painted necktie that matched the one worn by one of the jurors.

Interspersed throughout the article were quotes from famous judges and lawyers on the low level of jurors' abilities to understand, much less competently judge, a case. An example given to illustrate this point was that of a juror who asked to be excused in a personal injury trial. His reason was: "Well, you asked us to give $10,000 to your client, and I ain't got enough money to pay my share." Women jurors were judged to be "stonier-hearted than men in judging their wayward sisters." Women, at the time the article appeared, were eligible for jury service in about half of the states. However, if a presentable young man was on trial, women jurors were inclined "to identify him with a son or brother which is perfectly agreeable to his lawyer."

While the article was humorous in tone, it contained enough serious facts and examples so that the reader could not and was not expected to simply dismiss it. Its message was that the jury's verdict would depend more on the social backgrounds, observable prejudices, and characteristics of the jurors (all of which can be artfully manipulated by a skillful lawyer) and less on the juror's abilities to give responsible and competent consideration of the facts and issues presented during the trial. If you want justice, don't depend on the jury, find a good lawyer who knows how to manipulate it. In closing, the article stated:

> To many laymen all this psychological jockeying is vaguely disturbing; it seems somehow unethical. But lawyers point out that not all human beings possess ideal impartiality. Hence the lawyer's sweating and fuming over jurors is likely to remain an integral part of our judicial system. The assumption is that it all adds up to the greater protection of the client.[14]

A more serious and basic attack on jury competence appeared in the December 9, 1949 issue of *Colliers* entitled "Something's Wrong With Our Jury System."[15] The article was authored by Appellate Judge Jerome Frank. Frank's piece made many of the same points contained in the *Reader's Digest* article, only in this context they were defined as serious problems for which reforms were necessary. Citing numerous examples, Frank described how juries tended to ignore judge's instruction and make capricious decisions, how jurors' prejudices affected their judgment, how lawyers were able to successfully manipulate jurors, and how jurors tended to be influenced by what the press had to say about the case. Most important was Frank's assessment that jurors were often incompetent to make judgments concerning complex legal issues in complicated civil cases. His proposals for reform included drastically reducing or even abolishing the use of juries in civil cases, making jurors undergo mandatory psychiatric and aptitude tests, in many cases employing special juries composed of jurors who have specialized knowledge relevant to the facts of a case, and discouraging press publication of courtroom evidence during a jury trial.

The issue of jurors' competence was the subject of an editorial in the *Saturday Evening Post* of March 29, 1952.[16] The editorial was entitled "Why Do Solid Citizens Shrink From Jury Duty," and it reported the results of a survey for the Texas Bar Association that showed that of the 115,000 citizens in Texas who asked to be excused from jury duty, 82 percent were from the high-income group. Since most of those who asked to be excused were from the more educated, "better element," of the communities, the editorial expressed concern that individuals who were less qualified would come to dominate juries. "The odds being thus stacked against intelligence, the aged, the infirm, the busybodies, and the morbid hangers-on would fill up the jury box." The *Post* concluded

> The best remedy for the sorry state of the jury system is a decision by the so-called better element to get in and pitch. Deciding matters of great importance to litigants or accused persons—and also to a community's reputation for justice—is an experience that can't help [*sic*] doing a 'better-element' man a lot of good.[17]

Four years later, the *Post* ran another editorial on the question of juror competence.[18] This time it noted some of the reforms that had been made in jury selection. The editorial which was entitled "Informed Citizens Don't Balk at Jury Service," commended the success that the establishment of jury commissions in Illinois had in decreasing the numbers of excused jurors and assumedly increasing the prospective jurors' ability to function competently through orientation sessions. The 1956 editorial seemed to strike a somewhat different note on the issue of which types of people make good jurors than the one just referred to. It argued:

> . . . To those who feel that their education is inadequate, the jury commission explains that intelligence and integrity are more important than formal education . . . Before 1953, jury service was often the monopoly of a small revolving group of what might be called 'professional jurors.' Many of them were fine, public spirited citizens. Nevertheless, chronic jurors tend to develop a pattern of thinking which attorneys are quick to recognize and take advantage of. Conscientious amateurs, competently instructed in their duties, do a better job.[19]

By the mid-1950s the call for jury reform had become widespread and a number of states had established jury commissions to bring about change in the process of jury selection. Perhaps the most controversial of the proposed reforms was one that called for the drastic limitation or abolition of jury trials in civil actions. This proposal inspired a number of articles in the periodical press. One entitled, "The Case for Trial by Jury" by Caroline K. Simon, appeared in the *New York Times Magazine.*[20] It revealed an important shift in the discussion of the jurors' competence. In arguing for the retention of the jury system in civil cases, Simon noted,

> Faulty justice, it is admitted, lies not with the *quality* of justice resulting from a jury trial but with the *quantity* of cases which make trial by jury burdensome. . . . When we get down to cases involving real people, it seems an undue burden to trust one man, be he judge or

> other specialist. Most of us would rather place our fates in the hands of ordinary people like ourselves. Judges are learned in the law, to be sure and they have seen much of man in his many guises parading before the bench. And yet G.K. Chesterton's statement is still a truism: "I would trust twelve ordinary men, but I cannot trust one ordinary man."[21]

The question, then, became not so much the competence of jurors to judge complicated civil cases, but the lack of efficiency in the structure and operation of the jury system. It appeared to create numerous and burdensome delays and court congestion.

A major change in the jury system that began in the late 1940s was that many states which had previously barred women from jury duty were allowing them to serve. Perhaps it was only natural that the performance of women on the jury should be the subject of periodical articles. "The Verdict on Women Jurors" by Gertrude Samuels appeared in the *New York Times Magazine* in 1950.[22] On the whole the article made a favorable assessment of women's participation on juries. It noted however that women jurors have qualities that complement those of men:

> Women . . . are difficult to fool, especially where a woman's veracity is concerned. They appear to be less moved than men by large, glistening tears and beautiful orbs. They are largely embarrassed or bored by musical flights of oratory, preferring quiet documentation of evidence (this apparently goes for men jurors, too). And they are often slower to arrive at verdicts because they are less opinionated than men and because they have an innate sense of justice. . . . Lawyers for litigants in accident and negligence cases freely admit that they don't like to have women on these juries because they fear "penny-pinching verdicts." Jury officials confirm this view; they tell of women's frequently hard arguments with men to arrive at just verdicts on negligence or accident cases. . . . It is agreed that, since women have fewer commercial prejudices and intelligent calluses, they make fewer prejudicial judgments.[23]

A decade or so later, with the emergence of the Civil Rights Movement, the issue of black representation on juries came to the fore. *Life* carried an article, "From the Inside: Why the Finch Jury Disagreed," that described a jury's deliberation in a sensational murder trial that resulted in a hung jury.[24] Two jurors, a black and a Mexican-American, held out for acquittal while the other ten, all of whom were white, voted for conviction of first degree murder which carried the death sentence. The *Life* article described growing tensions that had racial overtones among the jurors. Based on accounts of the jury's deliberations that were provided by the white jurors, the two minority jurors were described as "being unable to understand the legal issues involved, at times emotionally unstable, monopolizing the deliberations, stubborn, engaging in 'violent and abrasive behavior,' and 'overly sensitive' on the racial issue from the beginning. It was like they had a chip on their shoulder." The two minority members, on the other hand, recounted incidences of their being excluded from information about housekeeping matters provided the other jurors during the deliberations. With regards to monopolizing jury deliberations, the black juror said, "one of the jurors asked a question on premeditation, and the foreman asked me to give my views. I talked, sure–but it wasn't a filibuster. There are some people who won't accept a Negro's view of anything." The picture that emerged from the article was that the ten white jurors competently fulfilled their responsibilities. It was the two holdouts, due to their incompetence both in examining the evidence and misunderstanding the judge's instructions, who were the problem. In looking back at their jury service, only one member, the black, said that he would be willing to serve on a jury again. Other jury members said:

> In my opinion there should never be a jury for a trial like this one picked from the rolls of registered voters. This type of case should be tried by superior court judges who know the law and are minus all sympathy and emotions and can decide the case on the evidence and the law.
>
> I think that's where the jury system is wrong; the selection of the jury. I believe the state should go into their personal lives, probe deeply and select people of intellectual ability to serve and then pay them decently for it. . . . Unless they make some pretty sharp revisions of the jury system, I would feel that should I ever be charged with a crime, God forbid, I would go to the judge and say, "I'll stand trial before a judge, but not a jury."[25]

The publication in 1966 of *The American Jury* by Kalven and Zeisel stimulated two articles in the mass circulation periodicals: *Look*[26] and *Reader's Digest.*[27] Both were written by Fletcher Knebel. The articles listed a number of popular myths about the jury that the Kalven-Zeisel study debunked: (1) the jury does not understand what it is doing, (2) the jury is putty in the hands of a skilled lawyer, (3) juries are incompetent because of the low educational level of jurors, (4) one man often hangs a jury of twelve persons, (5) a sentimental display on the witness stand influences a jury, and (6) the jury is trigger happy. The articles noted how the jury often tempered the demands of legal justice with a kind of ruthless common sense that included a tolerance for violations of laws that were often ignored, that is, game, liquor, and gambling, and a sensitivity to the larger context and implications of a crime. Knebel concluded:

> Perhaps the best testimonial for the American criminal jury comes from the men who studied it for ten years. They began their research without preconceived notions of the jury's role in the judicial system. They wound up as warm, admiring defenders of the jury. The jury, say the authors, agrees that ours is a government of laws, not of men. However, it also believes firmly in tempering the law with mercy.

> The jury, Kalven and Zeisel conclude, is neither as witless as it has been caricatured nor yet as noble. Rather, it is deeply American as the law's presumption of innocence—and they hope it stays that way.[28]

With the appearance of *The American Jury* and the comments about it in the mass media, the issue of jury competence seemed to recede and give way to the issue of jury representativeness. The lack of racial minorities and low-income people on juries became subject for debate particularly in the political trials of the late and early 1970s. Stories on such matters appeared as news articles in *Time*[29] and *Newsweek.*[30] (Perhaps because *Saturday Evening Post, Life, Look,* and *Colliers* had all ceased publishing.)

Closing on the same theme that introduced this section, we note that in August, 1967, the *Reader's Digest* carried a piece that contained a number of injunctions about how one should act as a juror: "Judge by the evidence, not by your heart," "Don't take the law into your own hands."[31] The goal of the piece was to instruct potential jurors about their civic responsibilities, what one must do in order to be a good juror.

A View from the Judiciary

Perhaps the most colorful attack on the jury is one that appeared in the *American Bar Association Journal* in 1924:

> Too long has the effete and sterile jury system been permitted to tug at the throat of the nation's judiciary as it sinks under the smothering deluge of the obloquy of those it was designed to serve. Too long has ignorance been permitted to sit ensconced in the place of judicial administration where knowledge is so sorely needed. Too long has the lament of the Shakespearean character been echoed, "Justice has fled to brutish beasts and men have lost their reason."[32]

But the most serious attack was the one launched by a distinguished member of the appellate bench, former Judge Jerome Frank. At the core of his criticism were his beliefs that the jury did not determine its verdict on the basis of the evidence, that members of the jury did not have the special skills and training that are needed to make rational decisions about the kinds of disputes with which they are confronted, and that juries were not motivated to carry out the tasks for which they were selected. In *Courts on Trial,* Frank observed:

> Again and again, it has been disclosed that juries have arrived at their verdicts by one of the following methods: (1) Each juror, in a civil case writes down the amount he wants to award; the total is added and the average taken as the verdict. (2) The jurors, by agreement decide for one side or the other according to the flip of a coin. (3) A related

> method, reported in a case where a man was convicted of manslaughter and sentenced to life imprisonment, is as follows: The "jury at first stood six for assault and battery, and, as a compromise, the six agreed to vote for manslaughter, and the vote then stood six for manslaughter, and six for murder in the second degree; it was then agreed to prepare 24 ballots–12 for manslaughter and 12 for murder in the second degree–place all of them in a hat, and each juror draw one ballot therefrom, and render a verdict either for manslaughter or murder in the second degree, as the majority should appear; the first drawing was a tie, but the second one resulted in eight ballots for murder in the second degree and four for manslaughter, and thereupon, according to the agreement, a verdict was rendered for murder in the second degree.
>
> How do the courts react to such a disclosure? When it is made known before the jury is discharged, a court will usually reject the verdict. But, frequently, the revelation occurs after the jury's discharge. In most states, and in the federal system, the courts then refuse to disturb the verdict. They say that any other result would mean that jurors would be subjected to pressures, after a case is over, to induce them to falsify what had occurred in the jury-room, so that all verdicts would be imperiled.
>
> One may doubt whether there is much danger of such falsifications. I surmise that the underlying reason for that judicial attitude is this: The judges feel that, were they obliged to learn the methods used by jurors, the actual workings of the jury-system would be shown up, devastatingly. From my point of view, such a consequence would be desirable: The public would soon discover this skeleton in the judicial closet. . . .
>
> "Mr. Prejudice and Miss Sympathy are the names of the witnesses whose testimony is never recorded, but must nevertheless be reckoned with in trials by jury." The foregoing tends to justify Balzac's definition of a jury as "twelve men chosen to decide who has the better lawyer."[33]

Frank referred to the opinions of colleagues and scholars who supported his views of the jury.

> My attitude toward the jury is not unique. James Bradley Thayer, a great legal scholar and a profound student of jury trials, said in 1898 that in civil cases, "I would restrict (jury trial) narrowly, for it appears to me . . . to be a potent cause of demoralization to the bar." Learned Hand remarked in 1921, "I am by no means enamored of jury trials, at least in civil cases. . . ." Mr. Justice Cardozo, in a Supreme Court opinion, wrote, "Few would be so narrow or provincial as to maintain that a fair and enlightened system of justice would be impossible without" jury trials. The noted historian, Carl Becker, one of the ablest students of American history and institutions, said in 1945: "Trial by jury, as a method of determining facts, is antiquated . . . and inherently absurd–so much so that no lawyer, judge, scholar, prescription-clerk,

cook, or mechanic in a garage would ever think for a moment of employing those methods for determining the facts in any situation that concerned him." Two very able and experienced trial judges, Judge Galston and Judge Shietag, have each recently indicated a belief that the use of the jury in civil suits should be severely restricted. Judge Shietag said: "The civil jury would seem to be unnecessary except in a few types of injury to the person, such as libel and slander, false arrest, and malicious prosecution."

Osborn, a keen observer of many jury trials, wrote in 1937:

"When a group of twelve men, on seats a little higher than the spectators, but not quite so high as the judge, are casually observed it may appear from their attitude that they are thinking only about the case going on before them. The truth is that for much of the time there are twelve wandering minds in that silent group, bodily present but mentally far away. Some of them are thinking of sadly neglected business affairs, others of happy or unhappy family matters, and, after the second or third day and especially after the second or third week, there is the garden, the housepainting, the new automobile, the prospective vacation, the girl who is soon to be married and the hundred and one other things that come to the mind of one who is only partly interested in the tedious proceeding going on before him. There is probably more woolgathering in jury boxes than in any other place on earth. . . . Someone has said that the invention of this jury system is one of the 'splendid achievements of civiliation,' but its splendor is now and then somewhat dimmed when some juryman frankly tells just what occurred in the jury-room. If for a term of court or two a complete transcript of all the comments, criticisms, and reasons of jurors in jury-rooms could be made and furnished to . . . the newspapers, it would no doubt furnish some suggestions looking toward improvement. If this exposure did not bring about the total abolition of the jury system, it would perhaps tend to bring about improvement in some of the methods of selecting jurors, or perhaps a selection of the kind of cases to be submitted to juries. . . . It is plainly said by those whose opinions command the utmost respect that the administration of the law in this land is on a lower plane than other phases of government and is unworthy of the civilization it poorly serves."[34]

Writing a decade or so later than Frank, Lord Devlin, a highly respected British judge, viewed the jury in laudatory terms.

Each jury is a little parliament. The jury sense is the parliamentary sense. I cannot see the one dying and the other surviving. The first object of any tyrant in Whitehall would be to make Parliament utterly subservient to his will; and the next to overthrow or diminish trial by jury, for no tyrant could afford to leave a subject's freedom in the hands of twelve of his countrymen. So that trial by jury is more than an instrument of justice and more than one wheel of the constitution: it is the lamp that shows that freedom lives.[35]

And in 1970 Simon Rifkind, a former federal judge, commented on the jury's independence as follows:

> It is not true that juries are rubber stamps for the judge. Anyone who has actually struggled with juries, tried to move their minds one way or the other, either in favor of the prosecution or the defense, knows that they are not rubber stamps. During the Prohibition era, you could not get jury convictions even though the facts were clear that the law against serving alcoholic beverages had been violated. We finally had to resort to padlocking the saloons in proceedings that dispensed with juries. Another example is of the husband who comes home and finds his wife with another man and shoots the intruder. There is no question that he has killed the other man and he tells the jury he did it because he wanted to save his home. Juries have been known to acquit in those circumstances. Juries have been known to acquit in cases of statutory rape when the defendant looks like an eighteen-year-old college boy and the victim appears to be a professional purveyor of her favors. But the best example of the independence of juries was given by Mr. Lefcourt: the hung jury in the Buffalo trial. And in the Chicago conspiracy trial, the jury found a verdict of its own.
>
> So, why do we need to abandon a system that is capable of such variety, flexibility, and pliability, and adopt one that is laden with defects?[36]

Among the most recent evaluations of the jury from a member of the bench was a positive one by U.S. District Court Judge Charles Joiner. In 1974, he summarized his opinions about the jury in the following five points:

1. I believe the decisions by juries properly instructed and taught are better than decisions by a single judge.
2. The principal reason for this is that the process of deliberation is a process through which the biases of individual jurors are exposed and isolated or controlled, and it is an ideal teaching procedure continuing throughout the decisional process.
3. Juries are better today than they were thirty years ago, largely as a result of the effort to make them represent a reasonably fair cross-section of the voting community, and as a result of the impact that television and easier transportation have had on their knowledge and experience.
4. Judges, lawyers, and court staff have a heavy burden to make the system work. All of them must make jurors feel at home in the strange environment of the courthouse by making certain the jurors understand everything they are asked to do.
5. Lawyers must not ask jurors to do more than they are capable of doing; in particular, jury trials of an extended case—unless it has major issues or matters of great moment or involved substantial personal liberty—should be avoided, because individual jurors have

> difficulty understanding why their lives should be disrupted for such substantial periods of time on matters that do not seem to be important to them.[37]

Most of the judiciary's evaluation of the jury, whether it has been positive or negative, has been based on hearsay and on personal observations. In a survey of 3500 trial court judges which formed the basis for their account of *The American Jury,* Kalven and Zeisel included the following item on their questionnaire:[38]

> Did you feel that the jury's verdict was:
>
> _____ without any merit
> _____ tenable for a jury
> _____ one a judge might also come to
> _____ quite correct

Seventy-seven percent of the judges found the jury's verdict at least accpetable.

In another national survey of trial court judges, respondents were asked which of the following statements best characterized their view:

1. On balance the jury system is thoroughly satisfactory.
2. The jury system has serious disadvantages which could be corrected and should be corrected if the system is to remain useful.
3. The disadvantages of the jury system outweigh its advantages so much that its use should be sharply curtailed.

The distribution of those responses looked like this:

Response Categories	*Criminal*	*Cases*	*Civil*	*Actions*
	N	*Percent*	*N*	*Percent*
Thoroughly satisfactory	791	77	661	64
Satisfactory if certain changes	210	20	280	27
Unsatisfactory	29	3	97	9
Total	1,030	100	1,038	100

According to Kalven:

> The tables require little comment. It is evident that the trial judges are overwhelming against sharp curtailment of the jury; and that this support for the jury does not decline appreciably as we shift from criminal to civil cases.[39]

Although these surveys were conducted about twenty years ago, there are no more recent data that either contradict or support their findings. We have seen that members of the judiciary who have spoken out on the subject of the jury do so in generally positive terms and none of them has taken up the attack launched by Jerome Frank against the jury.

Notes

1. Much of the material in this section was adopted from the chapter by Emily S. Watts, "Perspectives on the Function and Value of the Jury from American Literature" in Rita J. Simon (ed.), *The Jury System in America,* (Beverly Hills, Calif.: Sage Publications, 1975), pp. 161-177.
2. Ibid., p. 164.
3. Ibid., p. 163.
4. Ibid., p. 168.
5. Ibid., p. 163.
6. Ibid., p. 162.
7. Ibid., p. 169.
8. Ibid.
9. Ibid., p. 174.
10. Ibid.
11. I acknowledge with appreciation the help of Fred Fejes, a graduate student in Communications at the University of Illinois, in collecting the data for this section.
12. "Would a Lawyer Pick You as a Juror," *Reader's Digest* 47 (September 1945): 86-88.
13. Ibid., p. 86.
14. Ibid., p. 88.
15. Jerome Frank, "Something's Wrong With Our Jury System," *Colliers* (December 19, 1949): 126-128.
16. "Why Do Solid Citizens Shrink from Jury Duty?" *Saturday Evening Post,* (March 29, 1952): 110. Reprinted from *The Saturday Evening Post,* © 1952, The Curtis Publishing Company.
17. Ibid., p. 110.
18. "Informed Citizens Don't Balk at Jury Service," *Saturday Evening Post,* (August 25, 1956): 10. Reprinted from *The Saturday Evening Post,* © 1956, The Curtis Publishing Company.
19. Ibid., p. 10.
20. Caroline K. Simon, "The Case for Trial by Jury," *New York Times Magazine* (July 15, 1956): 12. © 1956 by the New York Times Company. Reprinted by permission.
21. Ibid.

22. Gertrude Samuels, "The Verdict on Women Jurors," *New York Times Magazine,* May 7, 1950, p. 22. Copyright © 1950 by The New York Times Company. Reprinted with permission.

23. Ibid.

24. "From the Inside: Why the Finch Jury Disagreed," *Life* (March 28, 1960): 76.

25. Ibid., p. 80

26. Fletcher Knebel, "How Good Are Our Juries," *Look* (August 23, 1966): 75.

27. Fletcher Knebel, "How Good Are Our Juries," *Reader's Digest* (November 1966): 239.

28. Ibid., p. 241.

29. "End to Peerless Juries," *Time* (September 27, 1968): 58.

30. "Twelve Missing Men," *Newsweek* (June 10, 1968): 58.

31. George G. Coughlin, "What Every Trial Juror Should Know," *Reader's Digest* (August 1967): 145-191.

32. Harry Kalven, Jr., and Hans Zeisel "*The American Jury*," (Boston: Little, Brown, 1966), p. 5.

33. Jerome Frank, *Courts on Trial: Myth and Reality in American Justice* (Princeton, N.J.: Princeton University Press, 1949), p. 108.

34. Ibid., p. 124.

35. Kalven and Zeisel, *The American Jury,* p. 6.

36. Simon Rifkind, "The Jury," in John Bonsignore et al. (eds.) *Before the Law* (Boston, 1974), p. 273. Reprinted with permission from *The Center Magazine,* a publication of the Center for the Study of Democratic Institutions, Santa Barbara, California.

37. Charles Joiner, "Perspectives on the Function and Value of the Jury in America from the Bench," in Simon (ed.), *The Jury System in America,* pp. 155-156.

38. Kalven and Zeisel, *The American Jury,* p. 429.

39. Harry Kalven, "The Jury, The Law and The Personal Injury Damage," in Rita Simon (ed.), *Reading in the Sociology of Law* (San Francisco: Chandler, 1968), p. 8.

Part II
Research on the Jury: Empirical Examination of How the Jury Functions

3 The Influence of Demographic and Social Characteristics on Juror Selection and Performance

There is no institution in the United States in which the notion of direct citizen participation in the decision making process is more clearly enunciated than in the jury system. But while the rules of jury decision making specify the importance of each juror's participation and the equality of the vote, it cannot guarantee the equality of influence in the deliberating process. Chosen as they are, most often from the voter registration lists of local communities, (in at least thirty-eight out of the fifty states) jurors represent diversity and heterogeneity. Differences in incomes, educational attainments, occupational skills, and ethnic backgrounds, are some of the major status differences that jurors carry into the jury room from the larger society. To what extent do these characteristics affect their performance and their interactions with fellow jurors? These are the major questions that this chapter addresses.

The chapter is divided into two sections. The first examines the relationship between the demographic and status characteristics of potential jurors, and the likelihood that they will be retained or challenged in the pretrial jury selection stage. Some of the most experienced trial lawyers claim that this stage of the trial in which the *voir dire* is conducted is the most crucial. The second discusses the relationship between juror demographic and status characteristics and their voting behavior on the jury. It summarizes the major findings concerning the relationship between those social characteristics and verdicts. It also summarizes the work that has been done on jurors' social characteristics and the amount and type of participation jurors engage in during the deliberations.

Representativeness

The U.S. Constitution provides for a jury of one's peers. In recent years, state supreme courts and the U.S. Supreme Court have had opportunities to define that phrase more specifically. Mr. Justice Murphy speaking for the U.S. Supreme Court in *Smith* v. *Texas* (1940) declared:

> The American tradition of trial by jury, considered in connection with either criminal or civil proceedings, necessarily contemplates an impartial jury drawn from a cross-section of the community. This means that prospective jurors shall be selected without systematic and intentional exclusion of economic, racial, political and geographic groups.[1]

A few years later in *Thiel* v. *Southern Pacific Co.,* the Court declared: "The American tradition of trial by jury . . . contemplates an impartial jury drawn from a cross section of the community."[2] The same standards were held to apply to state as well as federal courts via the Fourteenth Amendment in *Fay* v. *New York* and *Swain* v. *Alabama.*[3]

But, "nobody contends that the jury list must be a sample of the whole community," said Judge Learned Hand in *U.S.* v. *Dennis* (1950).[4] Hand went on to say that "not only does the law exclude those groups we have just mentioned (minors and the aged; the infirm and those of unsound mind), but it excludes those who do not satisfy the very modest financial minimum still retained; and those also who cannot pass an examination as to the other prescribed qualities—intelligence, character, and information."[5]

In the years that have gone by since Judge Hand wrote those words, the issue of the jury's representativeness became one of the topics for debate during the period of the political trials of the late 1960s. The jury was accused of having a positive bias toward middle America and a negative one toward racial minorities, the poor, the dwellers of the inner city, and the young. In 1961 the United States Commission on Civil Rights reported that total or partial exclusion of blacks from jury service was commonplace in the United States. The same Commission concluded in 1970 that "serious and widespread underrepresentation of Mexican-Americans on grand and petit juries existed in state courts in many areas of the Southwest."[6]

In a study of juror selection in the Eastern Division of the U.S. District Court, District of Massachusetts, 1970, Alker et al. found racial, age, sex, and socioeconomic class biases.[7] They reported that if "jury pools were to be representative of the entire residential population of the Eastern Division, blacks should represent 2.6 percent of the pool population, but in fact they constitute only 1.1 percent of the 1970 jury pool. In these terms they get only about 41 percent of their 'fair share' of jury pool places." The authors' explanation for the underrepresentation of blacks is the residency requirement on the voter registration lists. Blacks are more mobile than whites. They are less likely, therefore, to appear on the registration lists.

The bias against women showed up in a different way. They found that 54.1 percent of the names on the voter registration lists were female; but only 42.6 percent of the venire listings were female. The authors attributed the drop to a greater willingness on the part of the court to excuse females.

The bias against the young (those under 30-years-old constituted 21.3 percent of the population but got only 10.7 percent of the jury pool places) was attributed to "their underrepresentativeness on the voter registration lists."[8]

Using education as a proxy for socioeconomic status the authors found that persons with less than nine years of schooling and those with a postgraduate education were underrepresented; persons in the latter category, because they held positions (doctor, lawyer, teacher, and other professionals) that permitted them to be excused from jury service, and persons in the former category because their names did not appear on the voter registration list.

The authors concluded their report with a series of recommendations for implementing a fair juror selection process that would include the use of alternative lists to supplement the voter registration list, such as the census and police lists, and would sensitize court personnel so as to make them more aware of the types of persons who seek to be excused from jury service.

Attorneys Charles Garry and Dennis Riordin have suggested that if voter registration lists "do not produce a cross section of the community in which the poor or some other demographic minority are adequately represented, then social service lists should be used as well."[9]

In January 1975, the U.S. Supreme Court ruled in *Taylor* v. *Louisiana,*[10] that women could not be categorically excluded from jury service or given automatic exemptions based on sex alone. "The Court found that such exemptions result in juries that do not represent a cross section of the community, and thus violate the Sixth Amendment guarantees of a fair jury trial."[11]

In November 1978, the American Civil Liberties Union, acting on behalf of a criminal defendant (*Duren* v. *Missouri*), asked the Court to invalidate the Missouri System of jury selection.[12] While both men and women are called for jury service, under the Missouri system any woman may be excused simply upon her own request. Thus, the ACLU has argued that although women comprise 54 percent of the population of Jackson County, only 14.5 percent of the persons who have appeared for jury service are women. Tennessee is the only other state along with Missouri that automatically exempts women.

Almost all of the states have requirements similar to New York which states that no one may be excluded from jury duty because of race, color, creed, religion, sex, or national origin.

Jury Selection

In a talk before the New York County Lawyers' Association on the art of the jury trial, Louis Nizer observed:

> There are two schools of thought on the selection of the jury. One school says that it is best, once you have satisfied yourself that the jury does not know counsel or litigants and has no surface prejudice on the case, to waive further examination and with a grand gesture to say: Jury satisfactory.
>
> Many good lawyers do that. They hope to profit from the fact that the jury will say, "He has great confidence in his case, because he doesn't question as much."
>
> And then there is the other school, the school which says it is not given to you in other fields to pick your judges. You can't pick them in the

> state court, in equity trials, or in federal court. But the law gives you an opportunity to pick the judges of the facts. It is a precious opportunity and it should be used with all the resourcefulness at your command. I cast my vote for the second school.[13]

There is probably no area of jury behavior that trial lawyers believe more important or about which they believe they have more expertise than that of predicting the kinds of people who are likely to have the most to say and the greatest influence in the jury room. Trial lawyers are interested in the socioeconomic and sociopsychological characteristics of prospective jurors as a practical matter. They believe that selecting a jury with the right combination of social characteristics can mean the difference between winning and losing a case.

Prospective jurors can be challenged and excused from jury duty by either side or by the court for cause or through peremptory challenge. For a juror to be removed for cause, the lawyer for either side has to demonstrate why the juror is unsuitable. But in the matter of peremptory challenge each side has the right to ask a number of prospective jurors usually twenty to step down without offering any explanation.

As part of the Chicago jury project, a team of researchers interviewed thirty-nine trial lawyers representing plaintiffs in civil actions and defendants in criminal cases at the federal, municipal, circuit and superior courts in Chicago. These lawyers claimed that 50 percent of all their challenges were based on the juror's occupation (the characteristic most frequently cited) and on the juror's race, religion, or nationality. The next two most important considerations were previous injuries or claims of experience on the part of the prospective juror, and the lack of a sense of rapport that the attorney felt existed between himself and the prospective juror.

When asked to describe what they considered to be a prime function of *voir dire,* most of the lawyers responded by saying it was an opportunity to impress and get acquainted with the jurors and to sell their case to the jury. Some lawyers said they use the technique of accepting the first twelve jurors brought into the room, claiming that "mine is the kind of case that any fair minded, intelligent person couldn't help but decide in my client's favor." This technique is not only flattering to a juror, but considerably reduces the boredom which results in going from one juror to another repeating the same questions.

Others said they carefully observe the mannerism, facial expressions, and dress of the prospective jurors as they walk to the jury box, and, although they may go through the motions of asking each juror one or two questions, they have fairly well made up their mind before any words have passed between themselves and the jurors. While some lawyers try to pick those jurors who appeal to them personally, others on a more conscious level try to match jurors with the cultural background and temperament of their clients.

The degree to which the particular circumstances of a given case override considerations of general principles about certain types of jurors was emphasized by almost all of the attorneys. If an attorney believes he has a strong case, if he believes the facts are on his side, he will want intelligent, precise jurors, no matter which side he is representing. If, on the other hand, he believes the facts of the case do not support his client's claim, he will seek jurors expected to be sympathetic on grounds of identification rather than by a rational weighing of the facts. Both plaintiff and defendant attorneys stressed their fear of the "one-man" jury. Even though he looks as if he might be sympathetic to your case, there is always the chance that he might go against you and take the whole jury with him.

By going through the trial procedure literature, I was able to produce the following set of maxims that are representative of the rules of thumb lawyers are urged to follow. The first seven pertain to the lore that had grown up around women generally and older and younger potential jurors of either sex.

Age and Sex

1. A young juror is more likely to return a verdict favorable to the plaintiff than to the defendant.
2. An older juror is more likely to be sympathetic to the plaintiff than to the defendant in civil, personal injury cases.
3. A juror whose age closely approximates the age of the client, lawyer, or witness, is more likely to give a favorable verdict.
4. A women juror is more likely to be emotional and sympathetic and to return a verdict favorable to the plaintiff.
5. A male juror is more likely to return a verdict favorable to the plaintiff if she is an attractive female.
6. A female juror is more likely to return a verdict favorable to the plaintiff if he is an attractive male.
7. A woman juror is more likely to be intolerant to the complaints of her own sex and thus return a verdict unfavorable to a party of her own sex.

Clarence Darrow, one of the most famous trial lawyers of all times, had this to say about women as jurors. "I formed a fixed opinion that they were absolutely dependable, but I did not want them."[14]

For socioeconomic characteristics the guidelines seem to be:[15]

Socioeconomic Characteristics

1. A juror belonging to the same fraternal organizations, union, or political party as the client or witness is more likely to return a verdict favorable to that party.
2. A juror belonging to the same occupation or profession as the client will be more likely to give a favorable verdict. Modification: if parties of similar occupation are in close proximity, "jealousy" may influence a juror toward an unfavorable vote.

3. A juror belonging to an occupation or profession traditionally antagonistic to the occupation or profession of the client or witness is more likely to return an unfavorable verdict.
4. A juror who has or had extensive dealings with the public in matters of law enforcement and investigation is more likely to give a decision favorable to the defendant.
5. A juror whose occupation is that of a bellboy or taxi driver is more likely to be defendant-prone in a criminal case. They see so much of the frailties of human nature that they are not easily shocked.
6. A juror with a small income is more likely to be sympathetic with the poorer party.

For religious and ethnic backgrounds, the following apply:

Religious and Ethnic Background

1. A juror is more likely to return a verdict favorable to the party of his own religion.
2. A "mixed jury" will have a more difficult time agreeing on a verdict and is thus more likely to return a verdict favorable to the defendant.
3. A juror of Nordic, English, Swedish, Norwegian, German, or Scottish descent is more likely to respond to an appeal based on law and order and thus, to return a verdict favorable to the defendant.
4. A juror of Irish, Jewish, Italian, French, Spanish, or Slavic descent is more likely to respond to an emotional appeal and thus, to return a verdict favorable to the plaintiff.

About the above characteristics, Darrow offered the following advice:

> In criminal cases, I prefer Catholics, Episcopalians and Presbyterians to Baptists and Methodists, because the tenets held and the disciplines practiced by the latter set higher standards of human conduct and make them less tolerant of human frailty.
>
> The Irishman and the Jew, because of their national background, will put a greater burden on the prosecution and prove more sympathetic and lenient to a defendant, than an Englishman or a Scandinavian whose passion for the enforcement of the law and order is stronger.

In addition to demographic characteristics there is also some folklore about personality characteristics. For example:

> An intelligent, courageous juror is more desired by parties who feel they have a good case while a weak-minded juror is more desired by parties who feel they have a doubtful case and are dependent upon emotional, sympathetic appeals.
>
> A juror who adheres to defiant political or moral values is more likely to use non-legal sources as his basis for arriving at a verdict.

> A juror who claims strong opinions on any topic is more likely to be dogmatic and less able to bring various facts together for comparison purposes.

If one were trying to formalize and summarize the message about juror selection found in the legal cookbooks, it would probably read as follows:

> Groups traditionally believed to favor the prosecution as an agent of society include: (1) men; (2) Republicans; (3) upper income groups; (4) occupational groups such as bankers, engineers, and certified public accountants and others with positions of petty respectability and (5) members of the Teutonic ethnic groups, particularly Germans.
>
> Groups who are traditionally believed to favor the defendant are: (1) women; (2) Democrats; (3) middle and lower economic groups; (4) certain occupational groups such as social scientists; and (5) minority racial or ethnic groups such as Latins or Jews.[16]

On the basis of questionnaires filled out by several hundred jurors who served on civil experimental juries in Chicago, St. Louis, and Minneapolis in the late 1950s, we were able to draw a profile of the pro-plaintiff and pro-defendant type juror. Twenty years ago the prodefendant juror looked like this: He earned about $10,000 a year; he was employed as a clerk, or he was a businessman or a professional, he was of Protestant denomination and of Scandinavian, German, or "old American" ethnic stock, (that is, his family had been born in the United States for three or more generations). The proplaintiff juror generally earned less than $4,500 a year, he was a skilled or unskilled laborer, and his ethnic origin was Polish, Italian, Irish, Jewish, or Negro.

The underlying values that seemed to be represented in the characteristics cited above are ones usually associated with a minority or majority ethnic and religious identification, and an upper or lower class identification. Jurors who identified with minority ethnic, racial and/or religious groups are expected to believe that society's laws are superimposed by members of the majority and that they may be used to legitimate injustice. Such jurors are expected to emphathize with a party who is seeking redress of grievances for maltreatment especially if the complainant is a single individual and the negligent party a corporate body, and to have a generalized hostility toward what are defined as external symbols of authority. Finding in favor of a plaintiff and awarding higher amounts in damages is interpreted as an opportunity to express sympathy for an injured party and to demand a redress of grievances that carries with it the full backing of the legal structure.

Conversely, the following interpretations may be made about the meaning of a majority group identification. Such persons are believed to have more effectively internalized the values and norms that underlie the established legal code and to believe in their inherent justness. They are likely to have a stronger sense of identification with the established structure of authority, and a generalized respect for its external symbols. For such persons, the act of finding for the defendant or granting a lower award to the plaintiff, becomes an overt expression of their identification with the existing system of justice.

Although none of the trials used by the Chicago Jury Project involved straightforward criminal cases (only criminal trials involving a defense of insanity were used), on the basis of questionnaire responses from jurors who participated in civil trials, we hypothesized that jurors who were proplaintiff in civil cases would be prodefendant in criminal cases. In both instances, we reasoned, the jurors would be identifying with an injured or an accused party. Their findings of negligence or their verdicts of acquittal represent their disaffection with the accepted social-legal standards—thou shalt not transgress against the laws of the community and thou shalt not be rewarded by unearned gains.

We anticipated that the prodefendant jurors in civil cases would be pro-prosecution in criminal cases and would manifest their support for a strict interpretation of the established codes. The law to such jurors is perceived as the concrete representation of an external natural order that exists in the universe, and anything that threatens to disrupt that order must be punished.

Over the past decade or so, an interesting practice has been introduced in the *voir dire* of some of the more sensational trials of the late 1960s and early 1970s. The practice has been the presence of social scientists, that is, psychologists sitting side by side with attorneys, aiding them in the selection of prospective jurors. Jay Schulman, a sociologist, is perhaps the most well known of these consultants. During the Harrisburg Conspiracy trial Schulman and a colleague, social psychologist Richard Christie, conducted a study of the characteristics of registered voters in the Harrisburg area.

> Every *n*th name on the voting registration lists in the eleven counties in the court district was selected, and a short telephone interview was obtained with 840 persons, and certain nonsensitive demographic data were obtained. A sub-sample of 240 designed to represent the larger group was given a much longer interview (most of them in face-to-face situations) which elicited detailed information about media exposure, formal and informal group affiliations, general knowledge about political events, and a variety of questions designed to tap civil liberties ideology. This material was coded, analyzed and made available to the defense lawyers.[17]

According to Christie the lawyers were able to use the material in four ways.

1. In discussions with the judge they were able to use the material to argue for procedural points; e.g., according to our data the average voter in the district was almost 50 years old which is higher than the national mean: the judge opened the jury list to all newly registered voters.

2. They responded to the judge's request for possible questions for use in examining potential jury members by including all the items in our questionnaires, and much to our surprise they were accepted by the judge. The inclusion of these questions permitted a much more thorough examination of possible jury members. For example, the defense lawyers had not planned on asking questions about religious affiliation, which we found to be very important.
3. Our findings indicated that persons with certain combinations of background characteristics were extremely anti-civil libertarian. The lawyers were thus sensitized by questioning more intensively potential jurors with "bad" characteristics.
4. Schulman participated in the defense's deliberations on whom to peremptorily challenge and argued strongly and forcibly on the exclusion of potential jurors with a questionable profile.[18]

The jury eventually selected in the Harrisburg Conspiracy Trial voted 10 to 2 for acquittal on the major charges. The government opted not to re-try the case. In his comment "Some Reflections on Social Science and the Law," Christie reported that some months later a team of researchers interviewed the twelve jurors who tried the case as well as the twenty-eight who were preempted by the defense. He noted that "commonly accepted assumptions about the relationship between demographic variables and ideology which are valid in national samples are misleading when applied to smaller geographic areas." Christie added:

> Another finding which impressed us emerged from the interviews with the actual jurors. This was the seriousness with which most of them took the injunction to decide upon the defendants' guilt or innocence on the basis of the evidence. Several of them thought the defendants were actually guilty but that the prosecution had not proven the case beyond reasonable doubt and therefore voted for acquittal.[19]

Schulman and associates claim that they participate only in trials about which they have some ideological convictions and thus far have placed their expertise only at the disposal of the defense. In recent years, other individuals and organizations have developed strategies for investigating prospective jurors' backgrounds and making their findings available to either side. According to *Newsweek* (April 10, 1978), "In San Francisco, four companies sell 'jury books' containing files on jurors collected over the years. Former reporter Ray Carl McCleery who operates such a service, estimates he has records on 750,000 Bay area jurors."[20] At the time of writing a lawsuit is pending in which a prospective San Francisco juror, Godfrey Lehman, has charged that the state invaded his privacy by requiring him to accept jury duty and then allowing his background to be investigated.[21]

The selection was supposed to demonstrate that information about prospective jurors' demographic and socioeconomic characteristics, their political and social views, and personality traits are considered important to the outcome of a trial. In the next section we present data that describe the relationship between those characteristics and jurors' verdicts.[22]

Jurors' Social Characteristics and Verdicts

The first part examines the relationship between selective jurors' characteristics and verdicts in civil action. Legal cookbooks claim that the prospective juror's occupation is the single most useful piece of information for predicting whether a juror will be plaintiff or defendant prone. Data from the Chicago experimental civil juries did not show a significant relationship between the jurors' occupational status and their verdicts. Stephan reported that the only consistent relationship she found in her review of the research literature was that most jurors favored plaintiffs of their own occupational category.

Nagel and Weitzman reported that in personal injury cases predominantly male juries awarded higher damages to male plaintiffs than did predominantly female juries; and predominantly female juries awarded higher damages to female plaintiffs than did predominantly male juries.[23]

Snyder found that all male juries awarded more money in damages than did juries composed of both males and females.[24] Rankin reported two studies; in one, women jurors were more likely to find for the plaintiff than were men, but awarded less in damages than did the men. In the other, the opposite pattern occurred.[25]

Broeder found that awards in eastern courts were 40 to 50 percent higher than if the court was located in the rural midwest or the south.[26] Along these same lines Kalven and Zeisel noted that the larger the community from which the jury came, the larger the award granted.[27] Hermann found that registered Democrats were more favorable to the personal injury plaintiff than were registered Republicans.[28] Democrats, according to Hermann's results, assessed damages 8 percent higher than the national average while Republicans assessed damages 2 percent lower than the average.

Shifting to criminal trials, and assessing the impact of socioeconomic status, Stephen reported:

> In a study of defendants and juries from one hundred criminal trials, juries who found the defendant guilty had a higher mean prestige rating than did juries who found the defendant not guilty. In over 80% of the cases, there was a greater discrepancy between the defendant who was found guilty and his jury than between the defendant who was found not guilty and his jury. Reed determined that the socioeconomic status of civil jurors in Baton Rouge was unrelated to their decisions, but that higher-status petit jurors were more likely to find the defendant guilty than were lower-status jurors.[29]

The experimental criminal juries deliberating in defense of insanity cases did not produce consistently significant differences in verdicts among jurors of varying socioeconomic status. In the type of criminal case in which women are expected to be most punitive, the rape case, the evidence according to Rankin is that

> . . . although women tend to see rape as more serious and to sentence rapists to longer prison terms than men do, they are less influenced by the victim's reputation than men are, and appear only slightly more likely to convict.[30]

In the four studies she reviewed involving rape cases, Rankin found that women were slightly more inclined to convict for attempted rape, but in another case in which the evidence was weak, the majority of women jurors voted not guilty.

In the experimental criminal jury studies involving a defense of insanity, I found women jurors to be more sympathetic than men when the male defendant had been charged with housebreaking; but when the plea of insanity was introduced to a charge of incest, women jurors were more likely than men to vote for conviction.[31] In the incest trial, I also found a difference in the verdicts of women who worked outside the home and those who were housewives. The housewives were more likely to vote guilty than were the working women. Indeed housewives were more likely to vote guilty than were any other group of jurors considering occupational, educational, ethnic, and racial categories.

In both Broeder's work and my own, the relationship between jurors' race and verdicts was significant and consistent. Blacks were more likely than whites to favor acquittal. Broeder also concluded that jurors of German and British descent were more likely to favor the prosecution in criminal cases, while jurors of Slavic and Italian descent were more likely to favor the defense.[32] The experimental jury verdicts in general supported that observation, but the differences were not consistently significant. Stephan reported that Reed had found that in Baton Rouge (1963) "petit jurors with Anglo-Saxon birthplaces rendered more guilty verdicts than did petit jurors with French birthplaces."[33]

Experimental jury studies by Sealy and Cornish in England found the following relationship between jurors' characteristics and verdicts in theft and rape cases:

> The most striking aspect of the various results has been that an association appears in more than one of the different trials only between the youth of the jurors and their verdicts. The other positive relationships between attribute and verdict are not found in more than one of the different cases. The tendency of women to be readier to convict in the Rape case showed only in respect of the defendant Bryce; the tendency in the Theft case (Group 1) for the most elderly bracket to be readier to acquit than the middle-aged did not appear elsewhere; nor did the tendency of jurors having lower occupational and educational status in

> the Rape case to be readier to convict. The indications are that while such relations between group characteristics and verdicts may be predictable for a particular trial or sample of jurors the same effect may not recur if these factors are changed.[34]

This review of the relationship between jurors' demographic and socioeconomic characteristics and verdicts does not claim to be exhaustive. It does however represent the major themes and basic findings that empirical research on this issue has produced. What seems most striking about this review is its skimpiness, its tentativeness, and the absence of any strong support for many of the expected relationships and beliefs about how jurors of various backgrounds would in fact behave in criminal and civil trials.

Several years back, when I was analyzing the relationship between jurors' social status and verdicts in the defense of insanity trials, I observed that:

> It is extremely difficult to predict the response or behavior of a given individual to a concrete situation on the basis of such gross characteristics as occupation, education, sex, or age. In any situation what a person thinks or does is a function of who he is, the exigencies of the situation, how strongly he feels about the problem, and a host of other factors. In comparing jurors' verdicts by various status components we were not trying to predict concrete decisions. We were estimating the probability that some jurors would be more favorable to the defendant than others.
>
> What I found in that study was that the lawyers' . . . lore about the defendant-proneness of lower status jurors generalizes, although in a somewhat weakened form, to jurors' behavior in criminal cases involving a defense of insanity. For example, Negro jurors are more willing to vote for acquittal on grounds of insanity than jurors of majority ethnic background, and jurors of higher social status, as measured by educational attainment, are more likely to vote for a guilty verdict.[35]

I think, however, that the results of this most recent survey of research findings about jurors make a more dramatic point. That point is that the lore about how different types of people will react to the issues presented to them in criminal and civil cases is enormously more developed than are the facts needed to substantiate the lore. It is readily apparent from a perusal of legal cookbooks that date as far back as 75 and 100 years that lawyers, traditionally, have enjoyed playing amateur psychologist. Some of the most colorful members of the bar have written and spoken at great length about their intuitive or learned ability to challenge those jurors who are likely to cause their client trouble, and to retain those who will be sympathetic and understanding of their client's plight. They have worked out prescriptions that would fit almost every type of juror: the fat, the lean, the tall, the short, the smart, the dumb, the rich, the poor, the male, the female, the educated, and the ignorant.

In recent years, lawyers have obtained assistance from experts in human psychology. As mentioned early, Jay Schulman and Richard Christie represent a still relatively small group of social scientists who have placed their expertise at the disposal of lawyers whose clients have been charged with various types of political crimes and civil disobedience. Schulman and Christie make their services available only to those with whom they feel a sense of political and ideological kinship. But in addition to social scientists who lend their expertise on principle, there also exists today a practice of investigating potential jurors and of preparing "books" on them that contain as much information as resourceful investigators can uncover. These data books are for sale.

The purpose behind these efforts is the strong assumption that demographic characteristics, socioeconomic status, and political beliefs are powerful predictors of how jurors will vote in specific trials. Members of the bar believe that if they had enough information about each juror's background and status, they could predict with a high degree of accuracy how each potential juror would decide a particular case. They view information about who the jurors are as a valuable resource, and they believe that obtaining as much of that resource as possible would significantly diminish uncertainty and increase the likelihood that they will win their case.

The irony of all this is that these beliefs have so little basis in fact. The evidence as manifested by empirical studies shows that there is some relationship between verdicts and the jurors' personal and social characteristics, and that the relationship is in the expected direction; *but* the relationship is not strong. It is not nearly strong or consistent enough to merit as much attention and effort as the practice of challenging and selecting jurors has received from the bar.

Participation and Influence within the Jury

Two basic questions to which this section addresses itself are: Are some jurors more influential than others in determining the group's decisions, and if they are, which types of jurors are likely to have the greatest influence? Turning first to the Chicago experimental civil juries data, we note the findings reported by Strodtbeck and his collaborators in the civil trials.[36] In "Sex Role Differentiation in Jury Deliberations" Strodtbeck and Mann reported that men spoke more than women, and that women jurors played more passive and more expressive roles than did men jurors. Using the terminology employed by Bales and others who have worked in a small group laboratory setting, Strodtbeck and Mann found that the men on civil juries played more task-oriented roles and were more active in keeping the deliberations moving from one issue to another than were women jurors. Women were more likely to say things that reduced tension in the jury and served to unify the group. Hawkins also analyzed experimental civil juries. After he controlled for age and race, he found the same male-female differences as those reported by Strodtbeck et al.[37]

It is useful to remember that Strodtbeck's data were collected and analyzed in the 1950s, a period when most sociologists believed that the division of labor was such that men performed as breadwinners and as task-oriented leaders and that women performed as sources of nurturance, love, and stability. That this division of labor should also turn up in the context of jury deliberations was perceived as one more confirmation of the eternal and universal truth of the differences between men and women.

In addition to sex differences, another important characteristic that emerged from the experimental civil juries was the differential participation by jurors' in different educational and occupational status. Jurors who held more prestigious jobs and had more education participated more actively in the deliberations.

Table 3-1 which appeared originally in "Social Status in Jury Deliberations" shows that males talked more than females and jurors in more prestigious occupations talked more than jurors in less prestigious occupations.[38]

After the jurors had completed their deliberations, they were asked to answer a series of questions concerning their satisfaction with the deliberation and with the quality of the interpersonal relations. One of the items we asked was: "Which jurors do you believe contributed most to helping your group reach its decision?" We then identified the sex and occupation of those jurors and found the following relationship.

By comparing the distribution in tables 3-1 and 3-2, we see that the average number of helpfulness votes closely parallels the participation rates of jurors in various occupational groups—the higher status and more active participants were perceived as more helpful jurors. Within each occupational category, men received more votes than women. The correlation between votes received and participation was .69.

Table 3-1
Percentage Rates of Participation in Civil Jury Deliberations by Occupation and Sex of Juror

	Occupation				
Sex	*Proprietor*	*Clerical*	*Skilled*	*Laborer*	*Combined*
Male	12.9 (81)	10.8 (81)	7.9 (80)	7.5 (107)	9.6 (349)
Female	9.1 (31)	7.8 (92)	4.8 (28)	4.6 (62)	6.6 (213)
Combined	11.8 (112)	9.2 (173)	7.1 (108)	6.4 (169)	8.5 (562)[a]

[a]Numbers of jurors are shown in parentheses. Twenty-six of 588 jurors from the 49 juries used were not satisfactorily classified by occupation and are omitted. Since there are 12 persons in the jury, one-twelfth or 8 1/3 percent of the total acts is the pro-rata percentage for each juror's acts. This provides the baseline against which the effects of external status may be appraised.

Table 3-2
Average Votes Received as Helpful Jurors by Occupation and Sex

	Occupation				
Sex	*Proprietor*	*Clerical*	*Skilled*	*Laborer*	*Combined*
Male	6.8 (112)	4.2 (108)	3.9 (115)	2.7 (143)	4.3 (479)
Female	3.2 (34)	2.7 (116)	2.0 (36)	1.5 (76)	2.3 (262)
Combined	6.0 (147)	3.4 (224)	3.5 (151)	2.3 (219)	3.6 (741)

Source: Fred L. Strodtbeck and Richard Mann, "Sex Role Differentiation in Jury Deliberations," *American Sociological Review* 22 (Dec. 1957): 715.

The relationship between participation and occupational status generalized from the experimental civil juries to the criminal juries (the ninety-eight juries that deliberated on the two defense of insanity trials). For example, as shown in table 3-3 below, jurors who were proprietors and professionals participated more than did jurors who were laborers.

We also found, among jurors who participated in the experimental criminal trials, that educational status and participation were related such that the higher the education the more active the participation.

Jurors Education[39]	*Relative Participation (Percent)*
College	13
High school	8
Grade school	4

But the one status dimension that did not generalize across civil and criminal juries was sex. In the criminal juries, women participated as actively as men. Although no formal interaction process analysis was carried out on the criminal juries, listening to the deliberations could leave no doubt that the women participated as actively and as task-orientedly as the men. Indeed, as we indicated earlier, the verdicts of the women jurors, especially housewives, showed that as a group they were more likely to favor conviction than were jurors in any other status or ethnic category.

Jurors have one formal opportunity to confer a higher status on one of their peers. That opportunity occurs at the time they elect one of their members to serve as foreman of the jury. The information that they should do so is given to them rather casually by the judge when he instructs them on the law that they are about to apply, and on other matters pertaining to their role. In the

Table 3-3
Percentage Rates of Participation in Criminal and Civil Jury Deliberations by Occupation

Juror's Occupation	*Civil Juries* (48)	*Criminal Juries* (68)
Proprietors and professionals	8.9	9.1
Clerical workers	7.0	7.7
Skilled laborers	6.3	7.6
Laborers	5.9	6.1

Source: Rita J. Simon, *The Jury and the Defense of Insanity* (Boston: Little, Brown, 1967), p. 116.

experimental juries, just before they are escorted by the bailiff from the court to the jury room, the jurors were told, "At the outset, you are to select one of you to act as foreman of your jury."

Observations based on experimental juries showed that foremen were usually selected very quickly, in the first minute or two after the jurors assembled themselves. The first person to be nominated was most often the one chosen either by acclamation or by the absence of dissent. Hawkins reported that the second most common pattern was that the juror who began the discussion of who would be foreman was the person selected by acclamation.[40]

Although the process of selection was carried out quickly and casually, the juror who was elected foreman was most often the juror who sat at one of the ends of the rectangular table and was a person who enjoyed a prestigious occupation in the larger society. Hawkins found that among the forty civil jurors that he observed, three times more often than chance, the foreman was selected from among the jurors who occupied either the head or the foot of the table. (Jurors walked into the room singly or in pairs and were told by the bailiff to sit anywhere around the table.)

The occupational status of the foreman in sixty-nine civil juries and sixty-eight criminal juries is shown below.

We see that two and a half times more business and professional men were chosen in both the civil and criminal juries than would have been expected. A housewife was never selected, although chance would have predicted that ten of the foremen in the civil juries and five in the criminal juries would have been housewives.

Although women constituted 36 percent of the civil juries and 31 percent of the criminal juries, women were elected foremen 3 percent of the time in the civil juries and not at all in the criminal juries.

While there should have been 3.8 black foremen by chance alone, a black juror was chosen foreman once in the civil juries and not in any of the criminal juries.

Table 3-4
Choice of Foreman according to Occupation

	Civil Juries		*Criminal Juries*	
Occupation	*Observed*	*Expected*[a]	*Observed*	*Expected*
Proprietor and professional	31	12.5	17	7
Clerical workers	13	15.0	15	11
Skilled workers	16	12.5	1	7
Laborers	9	18.9	4	8
Housewives	0	10.1	0	5
Retired/unknown	–	–	2	1

Source: Rita J. Simon, *The Jury and the Defense of Insanity* (Boston: Little, Brown, 1967), p. 113.

[a]The expected number was computed on the assumption that all occupations would be represented in proportion to their numbers.

A general pattern that prevailed in practically all of the civil and criminal experimental juries was that the juror who was elected foreman talked much more than any of the other jurors. Hawkins reported that "the average participation for all foremen was 23.4 percent. The average for all jurors was 7 percent. In other words, the typical foreman talked as much as three regular jurors."[41]

For obvious reasons, all of the information reported in this section about differential participation in the juryroom has been culled from experimental juries. Direct access to the jury's deliberation in real cases is prohibited by law. But from sources such as the studies conducted by Dale Broeder, from interviews printed in the mass media that jurors have given after serving on an important case, and from the personal accounts that appeared in books such as *Juror Number 4*[42], the process and patterns described in the experimental juries seem to apply to real juries.

Concluding Remarks

This chapter traced the role of status characteristics from the selection stage to the deliberations. It examined the expectations and beliefs that the bar holds about the importance of such characteristics as the juror's sex, occupation, education, race, and ethnicity, in whether they will be successful in persuading the jury about the "rightness" of their cause. It summarized the relationship between status characteristics and jurors' verdicts, as reported by researchers who had studied the problem systematically, and found that there were only slight and not consistent differences in the verdicts jurors with different class, ethnic, and sexual characteristics reached. We reiterate that attorneys may be spending time and money elaborating on a process that has only slight empirical support and that can provide little practical help.

Only at the deliberation stage were there systematic and significant differences in the jurors' performance that could be attributed to their social status in the larger society. We saw that more educated jurors and jurors who held more important or more prestigious jobs participated more actively in the deliberations. They were more likely to be elected foreman and were more likely to be perceived as "helpful jurors" in getting the job done.

Notes

1. Smith v. Texas, 311 U.S. 128 (1940).
2. Thiel v. Southern Pacific Co., 328 U.S. 217 (1946).
3. Fay v. New York 332 U.S. 261 (1947), and Swain v. Alabama, 380 U.S. 398 (1965).
4. U.S. v. Dennis, 183 F.2d. 201, 225 (1950).
5. Ibid.
6. Bruce Johnson, "Inequality in the Courtroom: The Social Composition of Juries," Unpublished manuscript, 1976.
7. H.R. Alker et al., "Jury Selection as Biased Social Process: The Case of Eastern Massachusetts," *Law and Society Review* (Fall 1976): 9-41.
8. Ibid., p. 34.
9. Charles Gary and Dennis Riordin, "Gag Orders: *Cui Bono," Stanford Law Review* (February 1977): 582.
10. Taylor v. Louisiana, 419 U.S. 522 (1975).
11. Adeline Levine and Claudine Schweber-Koren, "Jury Selection in Erie County: Changing a Sexist System," *Law and Society* (Fall 1976), 52.
12. Missouri v. Duren, 556 S.W. 2d. 11 (Mo. 1977)
13. Louis Nizer, "The Art of the Jury Trial," *Cornell Law Quarterly* 32 (1946): 59-72. Copyright © 1946 by Cornell University. Reprinted by permission.
14. Clarence Darrow, "Attorney for the Defense," *Esquire* (May 1936): 212.
15. These Guidelines have been taken from Rita J. Simon, *The Jury and the Defense of Insanity,* (Boston: Little, Brown, 1967), pp. 98-106.
16. Michael Fried et al., "Juror Selection: An Analysis of Voir Dire," in Rita J. Simon (ed.), *The Jury in America* (Beverly Hills, Calif.: Sage Publications, 1975), p. 52.
17. Richard Christie, "Some Reflections on Social Science and the Law," Division and Newsletter, Division of Personality and Social Psychology, American Psychological Association (December 1972), p. 1. Reprinted with permission.
18. Ibid., p. 2.
19. Ibid., p. 3

20. J.K. Footlich, "Juror Privacy," *Newsweek* (April 10, 1978): 89.

21. Ibid.

22. For this section, I relied heavily on the materials in the chapter by Cookie Stephan, "Selective Characteristics of Jurors and Litigants: Their Influence on Juries' Verdicts," in Rita J. Simon (ed.), *The Jury System in America* (Beverly Hills, Calif.: Sage Publications, 1975), pp. 97-121.

23. Ibid., p. 102.

24. Ibid., p. 112.

25. Ibid.

26. Ibid., p. 113.

27. Ibid.

28. Ibid.

29. Ibid., p. 112.

30. Anne Rankin Mahoney, "Sexism in Voir Dire," in W.F. Hepperle and L. Crites (eds.), *Women in the Courts* (National Center for State Courts, 1978), p. 124.

31. Rita J. Simon, *The Jury and the Defense of Insanity,* p. 109.

32. Dale Broeder, "The Negro in Court," *Duke Law Journal,* (1965): 19.

33. Stephan, "Selective Characteristics," in *The Jury System in America,* p. 112.

34. A.P. Sealy and W.R. Cornish, "Jurors and Their Verdicts," *The Modern Law Review* (September 1973). Sealy's and Cornish's design was adopted from the Chicago Experimental Jury.

35. Rita J. Simon, *The Jury and the Defense of Insanity,* p. 111.

36. Fred L. Strodtbeck and Richard Mann, "Sex Role Differentiation in Jury Deliberations," *Sociometry* 19 (March 1956): 3-11, and Fred L. Strodtbeck et al. "Social Status in Jury Deliberations," *American Sociological Review* 22 (December 1957): 713-719.

37. Charles Hawkins, "Interaction and Coalition Realignments in Consensus Seeking Groups: A Study of Experimental Jury Deliberations" (Ph.D. diss., 1957), University of Chicago, p. 36.

38. Strodtbeck et al., "Social Status," p. 716.

39. Ibid., p. 117.

40. Hawkins, p. 23.

41. Hawkins, p. 131.

42. Edwin Kennebeck, *Juror Number Four* (New York: Norton, 1973).

4 The Rationality of Jury Deliberations and Verdicts

A major issue that this chapter addresses is how well the jury performs its job. Are the jury's verdicts consistent with the rules of evidence and law? Do the jurors understand the legal and substantive issues posed by the case? Do they understand the expert testimony, and are they capable of and motivated to adhere to the instructions they receive from the judge?

We commented earlier about the diversity of methods that the University of Chicago Project developed to answer some of those questions. Kalven and Zeisel sought answers by comparing jury verdicts against the decisions judges reported they would have made on the same case had they tried it alone.[1] Strodtbeck and Simon designed experiments in which jurors listened to audio tapes of edited versions of real trials and then deliberated.[2] The deliberations of several hundred criminal and civil juries were recorded. Broeder interviewed members of various juries in several jurisdictions after they had reported their verdicts and been dismissed.[3] He had each juror recreate his or her account of what transpired in the juryroom. The findings that emerged from these different approaches serve as a basis for this chapter.

We examine first the results of the Kalven-Zeisel surveys in which they compared juries' verdicts against the verdicts that trial judges reported they would have reached in the same case. The findings in *The American Jury* are based on the participation of 550 trial court judges located in different parts of the country. Altogether they reported on 3,576 criminal and 4,000 civil cases.

In each instance the judge completed a questionnaire detailing the facts of the case, the number and types of witnesses, the defendant's demographic characteristics (age, sex, race), the type of attorney (court appointed or private), the length of trial, and the specific charges against the defendant. If the defendant had a prior criminal record, the judge noted that as well as the nature of the prior offense. He also indicated whether the jury had access to that information. The judge also evaluted each case on the basis of how difficult or how easy he thought the issues involved were; and on whether he thought the weight of the evidence made it a "clear" or a "close" case. In determining difficulty or complexity, the judges were instructed to take into account the number of charges, whether codefendants were involved, the length of the trial, the presence and quality of expert testimony, and the legal instructions that the juries had to grapple with. On the matter of the evenness or one-sidedness of the evidence, the judges evaluated such issues as eyewitness accounts, types of physical evidence available, expert opinion, believability of the defendant and the witnesses, and the quality of the attorneys.

The most significant, and for those critical of the jury, perhaps the most unanticipated result of the study was the degree of similarity between judges' and juries' verdicts. In criminal cases, the judges reported agreement with the juries' verdicts 80 percent of the time; both agreed to acquit 13 percent of the time and to convict in 67 percent of the cases. In the 20 percent of the cases in which they disagreed, the jury was likely to acquit six times as often as the judge. Graphically, the results are shown in table 4-1.

Table 4-2 shows that the level of agreement in civil actions was practically as high, 79 percent. But the pattern of disagreement was evenly balanced. In the 21 percent of the cases in which judge and jury disagreed, the judge would have found for the plaintiff 10 percent of the time and the jury would have found for the plaintiff 11 percent of the time.

The jury's greater leniency in criminal trials is congruent with popular expectations, whereas the equality of proplaintiff-prodefendant responses between judge and jury in the personal injury trials is not. Popular beliefs about personal injury cases are that the jury is unwisely generous with the defendant's

Table 4–1
Percent of Judge and Jury Agreement and Disagreement in Criminal Cases

	Jury Found		
Judge Would Have Found	*For Defendant*	*Against Defendant*	*Total Judge*
For defendant	13	2	15
Against defendant	18	67	85
Total jury	31	69	100

Source: Harry Kalven, Jr., and Hans Zeisel, *The American Jury* (Boston: Little, Brown, 1966).

Table 4–2
Percent of Judge and Jury Agreement on Liability in Personal Injury Cases

	Jury Found		
Judge Would Have Found	*For Plaintiff*	*For Defendant*	*Total Judge*
For plaintiff	44	10	54
For defendant	11	35	46
Total jury	55	45	100

Source: Harry Kalven, Jr., and Hans Zeisel, *The American Jury* (Boston: Little, Brown, 1966).

or the defendant's insurance company's money. Juries were expected to be more likely to find for the plaintiff than judges; and certainly in those cases in which there was disagreement the direction of the disagreement should have been biased on the part of the jury being very much more proplaintiff than the judge.

The fact that there was 80 percent agreement and 20 percent disagreement between judge and jury permits critics of the jury to focus on the disagreements; and perhaps to claim that it is in those cases where the true test of the jury's intelligence, motivation, and rationality should be established. One might also argue, citing the 20 percent, that incompetent and irrational decisions should not be countenanced especially because in all likelihood they occur in cases that are the most difficult or in ones for which the stakes are highest. It is important therefore to focus on those cases in which the judges reported disagreements and try to understand the basis for the disagreements.

In *The American Jury* Kalven and Zeisel reported that neither the charges involved, nor the characteristics of the defendant helped explain the disagreement.[4] Indeed, after lengthy discussion of all the factors that did not explain the disagreement between judge and jury, they concluded that the most powerful explanation was the closeness of the evidence. We can describe that explanation graphically by distributing the criminal and civil cases in which there was disagreement into the categories in table 4-3.

These data show that the rate of disagreement was unaffected by the difficulty or complexity of the case (as witnessed by the 9 and 8 percents in column one) but that it was strongly affected by the closeness of the evidence as witnessed by the fact that in both difficult and easy cases, the percent of disagreement is almost as high 41 percent versus 39 percent. In other words, it is those cases about which the judges said "the weight of the evidence is so close that the verdict could go either way" that the judges and juries were likely to disagree.

Both pieces of data taken together then, the 80 percent agreement between judge and jury in criminal and civil cases, and the explanation that the

Table 4-3
Percent of Disagreement between Judges and Juries by Complexity and Closeness of Evidence

	Weight of Evidence	
Complexity and Difficulty of Case	*Clear*	*Close*
Easy	9 (618)[a]	41 (406)
Difficult	8 (57)	39 (110)

Source: Harry Kalven, Jr., and Hans Zeisel, *The American Jury* (Boston: Little, Brown, 1966).

[a]The numbers in parenthesis represent the number of cases in each cell.

disagreement inheres in the evenness or closeness of the evidence are powerful arguments for Kalven and Zeisel's unequivocal conclusion that the jury understands its job and performs it competently.

Experimental Juries

As discussed earlier, the basic thrust of the experimental procedure of the Chicago Jury studies was the involvement of real jurors who had been selected for jury service by the procedure typical for their community, and who listened to recorded trials that had been adapted from cases previously tried in the courts. These jurors deliberated and rendered a verdict. The juries' deliberations were recorded. A distinctive characteristic of the experimental method is that the same trial could be played before many different juries. In total, more than 2,000 jurors participated in five of these trials; three were civil actions and two were criminal cases involving a defense of insanity. The experimental jury studies focused primarily on the events inside the jury room: the topics discussed, by whom, at what length, and with what effect.

In *The Jury and the Defense of Insanity,* I noted that the jurors spent most of their time reviewing the court record.[5] By the time they finished deliberating they had usually considered every bit of testimony, expert as well as lay, and every point offered in evidence. The most consistent theme that emerged from listening to the deliberations was the seriousness with which the jurors approached their job and the extent to which they were concerned that the verdict they reached was consistent with the spirit of the law and with the facts of the case.

For example, the incest trial involved consideration of behavior that most people consider heinous and immoral. In their deliberations, the jurors said that they were seeking a verdict that would best prepare the defendant, his family, and the community for the day when the defendant would eventually return to society. The jurors spent most of their time trying to piece together information about the defendant's life, his job, his friends, his ties to the community at the time he was having sex relations with his two daughters in order to better understand why he did what he did. They then tried to connect the information they had about the defendant's early childhood with his illicit sexual activities. They discussed the various dispositions available to the defendant and tried to find a verdict that matched their own beliefs against the legal expectations of how people of the category of this particular defendant should be treated.

Jury Treatment of the Rules of Law

In their working paper "Methodological Issues in Simulated Jury Research," Colasanto and Sanders point out that many of the laboratory experiments that simulate jury decision making (Landy and Aronson, 1969; Efran, 1974; Izzett and Leginski, 1974; Sigall and Sotrove, 1975; Kaplan and Kerrerick, 1974; Nemeth and Sosis, 1973; Griffitt and Jackson, 1974) examined the effects of variables that were either irrelevant or marginally relevant to the law: factors, such as the victim's or defendant's attractiveness, that should have no effect on the jury's verdict.[6] Colasanto and Sanders criticized these studies, claiming:

> Thus, if a jury decides a case according to strict legal criteria these factors should not produce variance in jury verdicts. However, the results of most of the experimental work are that such factors do produce variance in the dependent variable. The conclusion one might draw is that there is a significant use of legally irrelevant criteria in the jury decision-making process.[7]

In their own experiment, in which they varied the rules of law, they found that:

> Although none of the groups of subjects conforms exactly to the legally correct model of the process of decision-making in this case, it is the difference in the degree of conformity that is important. The process of decision-making for deliberating jurors is closest to the correct model, while the process for the two groups of nondeliberating subjects diverges quite a bit from the legally correct model. Nondeliberators differ from deliberators most significantly because the nondeliberators tend not to use the criterion for decisions set out by the judge (intent instruction). The deliberating jurors and deliberating students differ from each other in two respects. Deliberating students are less likely to use their evaluations of the evidence within the context of the legal rules outlined by the judge and they are more likely to use legally irrelevant evidence concerning the identity of the victim in making their decisions.[8]

When the Durham rule was first adopted in the District of Columbia in 1954, one of the major criticisms leveled against it was that it would become a convenient vehicle whereby persons who had committed serious crimes could escape punishment for their behavior.[9] In essence the rule stated that if a defendant was suffering from a mental disease or illness at the time he committed the illegal act for which he was charged, and if the act was a direct result or product of his mental illness, he may be declared not guilty by reason of insanity. Critics of the rule were especially apprehensive because they recognized that in many instances responsibility for applying and interpreting the rule would rest with the jury and juries had acquired a poor reputation, in their opinion, for their failure to understand and properly apply legal rules. As indicated earlier, the basis for that reputation had not been established by a systematic evaluation of the jury's performance.

The Chicago experimental jury studies offer some data on the jury's ability to apply and interpret the rules of law in defense of insanity trials. To begin, a comparison of the verdicts reported by twenty-two juries who deliberated under the M'Naghten rule (which in essence states that if defendant cannot distinguish right from wrong, he may be declared not guilty by reason of insanity), as opposed to twenty-six juries who deliberated under the Durham rule for the same trial, showed that instructions made some difference. None of the juries that deliberated under M'Naghten compared to five of the juries that deliberated under Durham found the defendant not guilty by reason of insanity. The difference or the prodefendant bias as a result of using Durham as opposed to M'Naghten was 19 percent (0 out of 22 = 0 percent, 5 out of 26 = 19 percent).[10] It was not zero; but neither was it, as many critics of the Durham rule feared, 100 percent or even 50 percent.

Later, after the jurors had completed their deliberations, they were also asked which rule they would recommend that the courts use in the future, M'Naghten or Durham. Not unexpectedly the results showed a strong relationship between prior exposure and recommendation. For example, of those jurors who deliberated under M'Naghten, 37 percent favored M'Naghten, 26 percent favored Durham, and 37 percent said it made no difference. Of those who deliberated under Durham, 45 percent favored Durham, 28 percent M'Naghten, and 27 percent said it made no difference. But when these same jurors were asked to choose the rule of law they would request the judge to read to the jury if they were the defendant's attorney and wanted to obtain a verdict of not guilty by reason of insanity, the results looked like this:

As Defense Attorney Jurors Recommended	*Percent*
M'Naghten Rule	19 (112)
Durham Rule	49 (293)
No difference	32 (184)

Note: The numbers in parentheses represent the number of jurors questioned.

More than twice as many jurors recommended Durham as opposed to M'Naghten. Thus, when asked to step out of their role as jurors and into one in which they must identify with the defendant in the most partisan manner, the jurors appeared to recognize the prodefendant advantages of Durham over M'Naghten that members of the bench and bar perceived. But in their role as jurors they did not allow those advantages to influence their verdicts as much as their critics feared.[11]

Sealey and Cornish, who worked on the British jury system and used procedures they adopted from the Chicago Experimental Jury Project, reported:

> Our jurors behaved very much as did those who participated in the Chicago experiment. Our observation of the course of their discussions

> showed them to be deeply immersed, entirely serious, often vehemently argumentative, to all appearance oblivious that the situation was only an experiment.[12]

On the specific matter of the jurors understanding of and respect for rules of law, they reported:

> Contrary to common supposition, juries give real weight to an instruction to disregard relevant previous record wrongly admitted.[13]

Another approach that I employed for assessing the jury's understanding of legal rules was to compare jurors' responses to those of judges in the following context. A national sample of 400 trial court judges and fifty-four jurors in one community were confronted with the following situation.[14] They were told:

> In every jurisdiction in the United States, the *burden of proof* necessary to convict a defendant in a criminal trial is that the defendant's guilt must be established beyond a reasonable doubt.
>
> We would like you to do the following:
>
> Translate the phrase "beyond a reasonable doubt" into a statement of probability.
>
> Example: If you thought that there was a 5 out of 10 chance of probability that a defendant committed the criminal act for which he was charged you would place a mark on the scale drawn below as follows:

										X										
10	9.5	9.0	8.5	8.0	7.5	7.0	6.5	6.0	5.5	5.0	4.5	4.0	3.5	3.0	2.5	2.0	1.5	1.0	0.5	0
out																				out
of																				of
10																				10

> After the example, the judges and jurors were asked the following:
>
> What would the likelihood or probability have to be that a defendant committed the act for you to decide that he is guilty? Place your mark on the scale drawn below.

10	9.5	9.0	8.5	8.0	7.5	7.0	6.5	6.0	5.5	5.0	4.5	4.0	3.5	3.0	2.5	2.0	1.5	1.0	0.5	0
out																				out
of																				of
10																				10

The same type of problem was posed in the context of civil actions. Respondents were thus instructed to make a comparable set of judgments about the phrase "by a preponderance of the evidence."

The distributions in tables 4-4 and 4-5 summarize the judges' and jurors' responses.[15]

Table 4-4
Probability of Guilt by the Beyond-a-Reasonable-Doubt Standard

Judges			*Jurors*		
Probability	*Frequency*	*Cumulative Frequency (%)*	*Probability*	*Frequency*	*Cumulative Frequency (%)*
0.0–5.0	–	–	0.0–5.0	05	–
5.0	01	–	5.0	06	16
5.5	02	1	5.5	02	19
6.0	08	3	6.0	04	25
6.5	02	4	6.5	01	26
7.0	14	8	7.0	02	29
7.5	23	14	7.5	02	32
8.0	58	31	8.0	08	43
8.5	21	37	8.5	02	46
9.0	68	57	9.0	09	59
9.5	44	69	9.5	03	64
10.0	106	100	10.0	25	100
Mode	10.0		Mode	10.0	
Median	8.0		Median	8.6	
Mean	8.9		Mean	7.9	

Table 4-5
Probability of Negligence by the Preponderance-of-Evidence Standard

Judges			*Jurors*		
Probability	*Frequency*	*Cumulative Frequency (%)*	*Probability*	*Frequency*	*Cumulative Frequency (%)*
0.0–5.0	02	–	0.0–5.0	02	–
5.0	03	1	5.0	03	7
5.5	184	56	5.5	05	14
6.0	69	77	6.0	03	19
6.5	14	81	6.5	02	22
7.0	15	86	7.0	04	28
7.5	17	91	7.5	15	49
8.0	06	93	8.0	12	67
8.5	04	94	8.5	01	68
9.0	06	96	9.0	12	86
9.5	04	97	9.5	02	88
10.0	10	100	10.0	08	100
Mode	5.5		Mode	7.5	
Median	5.4		Median	7.5	
Mean	6.1		Mean	7.7	

We note that judges and jurors share similar definitions of beyond a reasonable doubt. For both, it means a high probability (above 7.5) but not certainty. But for preponderance of evidence, jurors appear to apply a more rigorous standard than do judges. For judges, preponderance means a little over the 50 percent mark (slightly more than even); for jurors, it means less certainty than beyond a reasonable doubt, but more than a slight edge. The judges thus make a sharper distinction between the criminal and civil standards than do lay persons.

Although the mass of data collected by Dale Broeder (about 5000 hours of interviews with jurors after they completed their deliberations) has not been as thoroughly reported as have other aspects of the Chicago Jury Project, what has been analyzed emphasizes the importance of personal experiences that jurors bring with them into the jury room.[16] Broeder's work stresses the importance of such factors as a juror's prior service, a juror's conceptions of family obligations and personal responsibility, direct knowledge about the trial that one gains from being a member of the community, and one's own set of experiences such as having been involved in an automobile accident, a victim of some fraudulent scheme, or of having witnessed police corruption. Broeder has written that such factors play important roles in shaping a jury's deliberations.

In his analysis of how damages are determined in personal injury cases, Broeder has argued that jurors tend to ignore relevant legal rules and rely more heavily on their perceptions of the plaintiff's family situation. In one case, a widow's benefits were lowered because the jury felt that she had a duty to remarry. In other cases, jurors relied upon their own experiences as drivers or passengers, or as victims of insurance companies' bureaucracies to interpret testimony in auto accidents. Standards of living and wage scales were also discussed on the basis of personal experience.

More than Strodtbeck and Simon, Broeder has argued that the jurors' personal experiences, encounters with the police, and life styles strongly influence their definitions of the situation, their perceptions of equity and justice, and their verdicts. But unfortunately, in the twenty years or so that have elapsed since Broeder collected his data, not enough of his work has appeared in print for others to gain from those materials.

Expert Testimony

Another basis upon which jury competency has been frequently demeaned is in its ability to understand and use the expert testimony as the law means it to be applied in the context of a trial. In the experimental defense of insanity trials, both the defense and the prosecution called medical experts to testify as to the sanity of the defendants. In the first trial the defendant was described as a psychopathic personality with psychoses.[17] He had a history of mental illness, suicide attempts, prior commitments to a mental hospital, and a medical discharge from the navy. The crime for which he was standing trial was breaking into and entering a private residence. He was found by the police crouching in the corner of an upstairs bedroom, his pockets stuffed with trinkets and jewelry of various sorts. The two psychiatrists who testified for the defense believed that he could not distinguish right from wrong (M'Naghten) or that (in another version of the trial) he was suffering from a mental illness and that the acts he committed were a product (that is, a direct result) of his illness (Durham).

In the second trial the defendant was described as suffering from a psychoneurosis that manifested itself in sexual perversions.[18] He had no history of mental illness or prior commitment to a mental hospital. He was not psychotic. The defendant was charged with incest. According to testimony given by two of his daughters, both of whom were adolescents, sexual acts between father and daughters had been going on for several years. During all of that time the defendant had held a responsible position in the municipal fire department and his wife, the girls' mother, had been aware of the situation. The two psychiatrists who testified on behalf of the defense said in one version, that in their opinion the defendant was unable to distinguish right from wrong, and, in the other version, that he was suffering from a mental disease and that the acts he had committed were a product of that disease.

In the housebreaking trial, 56 percent of the juries found the defendant not guilty by reason of insanity. In the incest trial 13 percent found the defendant not guilty by reason of insanity. In both cases the thrust of the psychiatrists' testimony was that the defendants were not responsible for their acts. On the basis of the verdicts, it would appear that the juries were more influenced by the psychiatrists who testified in the housebreaking trial than they were by the psychiatrists' testimony in the incest trial. But examination of the verdicts alone did not tell us enough about the jury's understanding of the expert's testimony. For that, we needed to examine the deliberations.

Typically, in the instructions the judge gives to the jury concerning expert witnesses, he tells it that a jury is not bound to accept the testimony of experts. He tells the jury that it should give to the testimony of experts such weight as in its judgment it is fairly entitled to receive. But, if the jury is satisfied that it does not accept the expert's testimony, it is not bound to do so.

In listening to the experimental juries' deliberations, we found that much of the jury's discussion focused on the problem of distinguishing between the expert's function and the jury's responsibility. The jury worked hard at resolving to their own satisfaction the problem of who should have final say about what happens to the defendant—a jury of laymen or a group of medical experts.

The following excerpts characterize the jury's dilemma:

> Is there anyone in this room that doesn't believe in psychiatry? That's the whole thing in my estimation. It's whether or not you are going to take the word of these two men, who are well known and are admired in the field, and have excellent jobs. They are impartial. They're working for the county hospital. Are you going to take their word, or are you going to sit there and say that we know. We don't even know this man. They worked with him, they both say that he is mentally disturbed. If you don't take that as proof, I don't know what you are going to do. I mean to me, in other words, if you don't find him not guilty by reason of insanity, you're sitting here disregarding the two psychiatrists in the case.

A few minutes later, in the same deliberations, another juror responded.

> What I'm trying to say is just because these people are educated and they are way up over our heads that we have to accept what they say as truth and that's it. In other words, they would be deciding for us, then we are not deciding for ourselves what is right in this particular case.

A third juror interrupted to agree:

> If that's the case, this case shouldn't ever have gone to a jury. I mean that we should have to depend upon men specialized in the field of psychiatry to judge this man.

The second juror continued:

> That's right, you don't need a jury if you are going to take two doctors' words and say that this man is insane. Why do you need a jury?[19]

During the trial, in cross-examination both defense psychiatrists had insisted that insanity was a judicial term and involved a determination which they did not feel qualified to make. This statement was the source of considerable puzzlement in practically every deliberation. One juror expressed it this way:

> What I don't clearly understand is are we talking in terms of legal insanity; or technical insanity; or medical insanity, the jargon of the psychiatrists? In the jargon of the psychiatrists, they do not declare him insane; they do not associate this man with the term that they generally associate with insanity, people who do not have control over their actions. The word psychosis came up, but they do not identify this man with having a psychosis, he had a mental disorder.

Later in the deliberation the same juror commented:

> My argument is that the experts do not associate a mental illness to this man that has significance in terms of insanity. He had a mental disorder but was it such that the man was not responsible for his actions?[20]

A problem that is especially interesting to trial lawyers is how jurors assimilate conflicting expert opinions; and how in turn this reflects on the status of the expert witnesses. Phrased differently the problem becomes, can testimony that has been tinged by partisanship nevertheless reflect the accumulated knowledge represented by the particular discipline? The following excerpts illustrate how jurors reacted to conflicting testimony in the experimental trials.

> You understand that there are apparently four different schools of psychiatry, all of whom claim their school was right and the other school was wrong; and, although they have made progress in psychiatry, I don't think they identified it as a precise science as yet.

Another juror distinguished the testimony of each side in the following way:

> The big factor in my mind was that the two psychiatrists who testified that he was mentally deranged really examined the defendant. The other one—I think the other man was a brilliant man, probably, but the other man definitely had *not* examined this particular gentleman. I would have thought a lot more of his testimony, I mean, I see no reason for disbelieving him, but I would have thought a lot more of his testimony if he had examined him. The other two doctors had examined him and that's an important difference in my opinion.[21]

Another source of controversy about psychiatric testimony is the fear that the psychiatrists' prestige will cause jurors to lose faith in their own role in the proceedings. To find out about that, we formulated the issues as follows: How do jurors, as representatives of the general public, react to the idea of relinquishing their responsibility for deciding cases involving a defense of insanity? After the deliberations were over, the jurors were asked:

> Which to you is the best way of deciding what should be done with a person who has committed a crime and pleads that he is insane?
>
> _____ He should be tried before a jury, just like anyone else.
> _____ He should be tried before a judge.
> _____ He should be turned over by the court to psychiatrists and they should determine what is to be done with him.

Only 7 percent selected the judge. The choice then was between a jury of laymen or a group of medical experts, and between them the jury was favored almost two to one. Of the one-third who were willing to delegate authority to the psychiatrists, the majority were jurors who had found the defendant not guilty by reason of insanity. But the point to be emphasized is that two-thirds were not prepared to relinquish their responsibility to an expert body. The following comment from one of the deliberations captures some of the feelings surrounding this point:

> The judge said that we could disregard their testimony, if we wanted to. After all, you can't base your whole opinion on the fact that these people have degrees.[22]

In one of the experimental jury studies involving the defense of insanity, half of the juries were given no information about what the defendant's fate would be if they should find him not guilty by reason of insanity. In fact, in most states and in all federal jurisdictions, a person who is acquitted on grounds on insanity is immediately confined to a mental institution until medical authorities determine that he or she is recovered or is restored to sanity. In some jurisdictions, however, the jury is not instructed as to what the consequences of a not-guilty by-reason-of-insanity verdict would be. Some lawyers believe that jurors assume that the defendant would go free and they argue that the lack of information prejudices the defendant's right to acquittal. They reason that a jury is not likely to tolerate releasing a person who had violated the legal and moral code of the community and who might repeat the act.

In the design of the housebreaking trial, half of the juries were instructed by the judge that if they should find the defendant not guilty by reason of insanity, he would be committed to a mental institution until such time as hospital authorities authorized his release. The other juries were given no information about the possible consequences of a not guilty by reason of insanity verdict. In the percentages that appear in table 4-6 we see that distribution of verdicts was almost identical between the two sets of juries.

The absence of commitment information did not increase, to any significant extent, the likelihood that a jury would find the defendant guilty nor did the

Table 4-6
Commitment Information by Jury Verdicts

	Commitment Information	
Jury Verdicts	*Present*	*Absent*
Not guilty by reason of insanity	9	8
Guilty	2	3
Hung	4	4
Total	15	15

Source: Rita J. Simon, *The Jury and the Defense of Insanity* (Boston: Little, Brown, 1967), p. 92.

presence of information enhance the likelihood that the jury would acquit the defendant on grounds of insanity.

But there may be some puzzle as to how to interpret the lack of differences between the two treatments. Perhaps the jury is after all not concerned with the defendant's disposition? Or perhaps the jury somehow determines by itself, in the absence of specific information, that the court will provide for some period of commitment before it allows the defendant to go free?

We have information bearing on both hypotheses. After the deliberations, the jurors were asked:[23]

> In a criminal case like this one, what do you think happens to the defendant when the jury returns a verdict of not guilty by reason of insanity?
>
> The alternatives were:
>
> ____He is put in a mental institution for a period of time set by the court.
> ____He is put in a mental institution until, in the opinion of the psychiatrists, he is cured.
> ____He is put in prison.
> ____He is placed on probation.
> ____He is set free.

This question was put to all jurors, those who were given the commitment instruction and those who were not. Ideally, all jurors who were exposed to the commitment instruction version should have checked "He is put in a mental institution until, in the opinion of the psychiatrists, he is cured." But table 4-7 shows that 93 percent of the jurors who received the commitment information

Table 4-7
Jurors' Expectations about the Court's Disposition of the Defendant by Commitment Instruction

Commitment Instruction	*Mental Institution*[a]	*Prison (%)*	*Probation or Free*	*Combined (N = 180)*
Given	93	3	4	100
Not given	91	3	6	100

Source: Rita J. Simon, *The Jury and the Defense of Insanity* (Boston: Little, Brown, 1967), p. 94.

[a]Of those respondents who checked "mental institution," 20 percent (in both treatments) indicated that they believed the length of time defendant remained in the institution was designated by the court. The remaining 71 or 73 percent of the jurors indicated that they believed the defendant "is put in a mental institution until, in the opinion of the psychiatrists, he is cured."

checked the correct answer, and 91 percent who did *not* receive the information also checked the "commitment to mental institution" alternative. Thus we see that jurors who did not receive the commitment instruction assumed correctly that the defendant would be committed.

How Consensus Is Reached in the Juryroom

How often do jurors enter the juryroom divided in their beliefs about the defendant's guilt, compared to entering with consensus, even before deliberations begin? Which pattern is more prevalent: one in which most people have formed an opinion before they enter the juryroom and their opinions remain unchanged by what is said during the deliberations, or one in which most people are undecided before they begin to deliberate and the subsequent discussion determines their final decision?

One technique that was used to answer this question among experimental juries was to compare the jurors' individual verdicts as reported on questionnaires immediately after the trial but before the deliberations began, against the group's decision, and then to compare both verdicts against individual verdicts reported on a questionnaire following the group discussion. The results indicated that among 55 percent of the jurors there was no conflict between the opinions they held before they entered the jury room and the subsequent group decision. In other words, more than half the jurors formed an opinion before the deliberations began; and that opinion did not change as a result of the group discussion. An additional 16 percent were in juries that were unable to reach a consensus. They reported themselves as hung juries. The full pattern is described below in table 4-8. Note that of the 16 percent in hung juries, 12 had formed opinions before the deliberation began and were not sufficiently moved by what was said in the discussion to change their opinions. Thus, a total of 67 percent of the jurors (55 percent of those in groups that reached consensus before the deliberations began plus an additional 12 percent in the hung juries) would have reached the same decision if there had never been a deliberation; in other words, if the court had polled the jurors individually right after the trial. For 23 percent, the group discussion was significant. It changed their previously held individual verdicts and made them consistent with the majority. This was the case even for the 4 percent who were in hung juries where the majority of the juries' verdicts matched the verdicts reported by those individuals who shifted their verdicts. All of these jurors apparently did have a true change of belief and were not responding to group pressure, because when they were given the opportunity to state privately what their verdicts were, they reported the same opinions as that reached by the group.

Of the remaining 10 percent, 70 percent went along with the majority, but probably because they wanted to avoid a hung jury. Afterward in private, they

Table 4-8
Relationship between Individual and Group Decisions

Predeliberation Individual Verdicts	*Verdict Reported by the Jury*	*Postdeliberation Individual Verdicts*	*Percent of Jurors*
NGI[a]	NGI	NGI	5
Guilty	Guilty	Guilty	50
NGI	Hung	NGI	3
Guilty	Hung	Guilty	9
NGI	Hung	Guilty	3
Guilty	Hung	NGI	1
NGI	Guilty	Guilty	15
Guilty	NGI	NGI	4
NGI	Guilty	NGI	5
Guilty	NGI	Guilty	2
NGI	NGI	Guilty	2
Guilty	Guilty	NGI	1

Source: Rita J. Simon, *The Jury and the Defense of Insanity* (Boston: Little, Brown, 1967), p. 64.

[a]NGI = not guilty by reason of insanity.

gave their original opinion which was one that opposed the verdict reached by the group. The other 30 percent shifted their verdicts in such a manner as to question whether they understood what was happening. But remember they constitute only 3 percent of all the jurors. Thus, for the 816 jurors described in table 4-8 the results show that in slightly more than one out of three juries the group verdicts differed from those which the jurors would have reported if they were polled individually immediately following the trial.

Unlike the situation portrayed so dramatically in the movie *Twelve Angry Men,* it is extremely rare for one juror to hang the jury. In almost every instance in which there was a hung jury among the experimental civil and criminal juries, the size of the coalitions were six to six, seven to five, or eight to four. In groups that reached consensus, in only about one in ten times did a minority coalition succeed in convincing a majority of the jurors to accept its point of view. Among that 10 percent, the size of the minority was most often five. There were no instances in which one juror or even two held out against the other ten or eleven and then succeeded in persuading them to their position.

The data from the experimental juries closely match comparable information collected by Zeisel and Broeder in interviews with some 2,500 jurors who sat on real cases in Chicago and Brooklyn.[24] They were asked to describe the distribution of votes on the first ballot in the jury room. For each jury, the first ballot votes were then compared against the jury's verdict. Table 4-9 shows the relationship between first ballots, which were taken before there was any substantive discussion of the case, and group verdicts.

Table 4-9
First Ballot Votes by Jury Verdicts

	Guilty Votes on First Ballot (%)				
Final Verdict	*0*	*1-5*	*6*	*7-11*	*12*
Not guilty	100	91	50	5	–
Hung	–	7	–	9	–
Guilty	–	2	50	86	100
Total	100	100	100	100	100
Number of cases	26	41	10	105	43

Source: Rita J. Simon, *The Jury and the Defense of Insanity* (Boston: Little, Brown, 1967), p. 489.

In referring to the data in table 4-9, Kalven and Zeisel commented:

> . . . in the instances where there is an initial majority either for conviction or for acquittal, the jury in roughly nine out of ten cases decides in the direction of the initial majority. Only with extreme infrequency does the minority succeed in persuading the majority to change its mind during the deliberation. But this is only to say that *with very few exceptions the first ballot decides the outcome of the verdict.* And if this is true, then *the real decision is often made before the deliberation begins.*[25]

Consider the first ballot votes as comparable to the predeliberation verdicts, and then note that the two sets of data (those from the experimental juries and those based on interviews with jurors who served on real cases) make the same point. Much of the time the deliberation does not decide the case. In other words, if the jurors were polled individually immediately following the trial and the majority opinion adopted as the group's decision, that verdict would match the verdict the jury eventually reports as its unanimous decision about 80 percent of the time.

There are those who claim, however, that it is in just that small proportion of cases in which the minority view does prevail that a person's life or entire future is likely to be at stake. They claim that cases in which the minority is successful are not randomly distributed but are indeed the most important cases because a principle or a life is on trial. Kalven and Zeisel commented:

> Perhaps [the deliberation] does not so much decide the case as bring about the consensus, the outcome of which has been made highly likely by the distribution of first ballot votes. The deliberation process might well be likened to what the developer does for an exposed film: it brings out the picture, but the outcome is pre-determined.[26]

For his doctoral dissertation Charles Hawkins studied interaction and coalition realignment in juries, using the experimental jury tapes[27] (see figure 4-1). He had access to sixty-nine jury deliberations based on a civil action involving the personal injury of a baby.

In his analysis of the social process of the deliberations, Hawkins commented:

> . . . once a coalition had acquired a single new adherent from the opposing coalition, it was never in danger of losing the verdict. After some of the opponents had switched, the remaining members might stand fast, forcing the jury into a stalemate. However, once the gaining coalition had added one person to their side, there was never an instance where they subsequently all switched over to the opponent's side. The surprising conclusion from this finding is that the first juror to switch his vote will indicate by his move the only possible verdict the jury can reach!
>
> Admittedly this finding must be supported by additional evidence before it can be accepted as conclusive. Nevertheless, in our juries the pattern is so consistent that we are safe in concluding that the trend toward consensus is extremely strong. The phenomena of double switching jurors and of compensating vote switches on a given poll must be quite rare. This means that the process of consensus-seeking in juries aligned in coalitions can be viewed as essentially a process of removing obstacles in the path of attaining unanimity. Once the direction of movement is fixed, the jury's only job is to keep the movement going and not to let it get hung up on the obstinacy of the remaining minority jurors. It is for this reason that we used the term "coalition *re*alignments" in the title of the dissertation rather than "coalition alignments." The job of the jury is to cause realignments or vote switches of the members. The gaining coalition works to get them; the losing coalition works to stop them.
>
> When the jury is divided openly into two opposing coalitions, the contention is no longer between twelve separate individuals but between only two collectivities. When one person speaks, he acts as a representative of a subgroup rather than as an advocate of a single opinion. The other members of the coalition need not worry as long as they can feel confident that the speaker is making a strong attack upon the opponents and a strong defense on their side of the issue. The fact that he may not put the arguments to the opponents in just the same way that they would is no reason for worrying, unless they perceive loopholes in his arguments which might endanger their side.
>
> In this situation, the strength of each side depends upon their ability to sustain a consistent verbal attack. The jury feels that they are progressing only as long as the two sides continue to defend themselves or attack the opponents. The interaction between the coalitions will tend to be balanced, regardless of their size. We found that the amount of intereaction initiated by a coalition tended to be inflated in inverse ratio to its size. Because interaction in this situation becomes a matter of the pure exercise of power, the ability of the minority coalition to

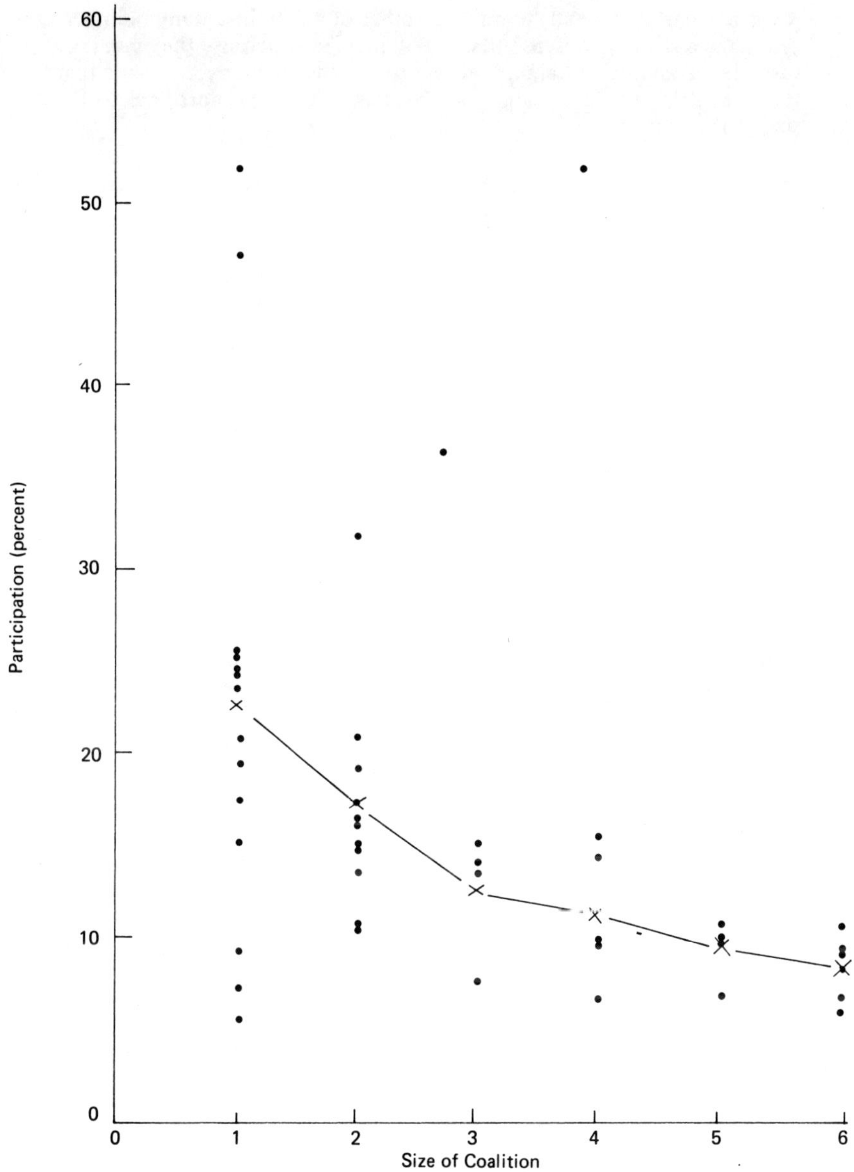

Combined Average Participation per Member:

22.8	17.1	12.5	11.3	9.4	8.3

Ratio to Expected (1/12th):

2.7	2.0	1.5	1.4	1.1	1.0

Source: From Charles Hawkins, "Interaction and Coalition Realignments in Consensus Seeking Groups: A Study of Experimental Jury Deliberations" (Ph.D. diss. University of Chicago, 1957). Reprinted with permission.

Figure 4–1. Average Participation per Member of a Coalition, Sizes One to Six (Minority Coalitions Only)

resist persuasion depends upon its number of adherents. Many members can make a stronger defense than a few members, because they can take turns in sustaining the argument. We found that the length of time that the vote split would remain constant was directly proportional to the size of the minority.[28]

Hawkins also reported an inverse relationship between jurors' participation and size of coalition. On the average he found that

> . . . minorities of one talk 2.7 times as much as would be expected on the basis of chance. In other words, a single juror facing a majority of eleven talks almost as much as would be expected of three men. Minorities of two talk exactly 2.0 times as much as would be expected. In other words, they initiate as much interaction as would be expected from four jurors. The ratio of observed to expected is above one for all minority coalitions. The combined average participation per member for all minority coalitions from size one to size five plus the seven coalitions of size six shown in Figure 4 is 12.4 percent.[29]

Hawkins continued:

> . . . in many situations it can be assumed that the time of the group is a scarce resource which must be allocated among the potential speakers, much as any other economic commodity. In juries, however, when one is in a small minority, it is not necessarily an advantage to be able to speak. Knowing that anything you say will be immediately contradicted by most of the group and that few if any people will come to your defense, you may very well prefer to remain silent. Participation is not necessarily rewarding under these circumstances.
>
> Moreover, it is clear from the deliberations that the majority uses this principle to tactical advantage. The reason that participation tends to be balanced between coalitions is in part due to the fact that the majority *forces* the minority jurors to respond. They demand that the minority talk. There are several devices for doing this. In the first place, juries appear to deliberate with an implicit norm that it is the obligation of the minority to defend its views. The presumption of correctness lies with the majority. Therefore, the minority view cannot be given credit unless it is actively argued. The reader may recall that a similar norm was sometimes used in "one-sided" voting, where either the pro plaintiff or the pro defendant jurors, but not both, were asked to indicate their vote: the side asked to vote was the one presumed to be in the minority.
>
> The majority jurors may use harassing tactics to draw out the minority. Many different jurors are brought into the argument, but each speech is of short duration. It can sometimes come to the point where the majority jurors begin to interrupt one another so that each one can get in his licks. The majority jurors who have carried the burden of the argument in the earlier stages, when the relative strengths of the opposing factions were as yet unclear, may retire and turn over the attack to the other members.

> The pressure by the majority to draw the minority into active argument is also shown in some cases by the content of their assertions. When the minority may not respond to a mildly opinionated view, a strongly slanted argument may goad them into action. Thus, where there is a stable situation, with two contending coalitions facing each other without changes of alignment, the arguments of the majority may become more and more extreme. They make assertions that even they themselves would not have believed earlier in the discussion.[30]

Using the technique of the Chicago experimental jury studies on juries in which the unanimity rule did not apply, Kessler observed that even though a jury had reached a verdict, the majority continued to press the minority members to explain why they disagreed with them and tried to bring them into the majority camp.[31] But Kessler also reported that if the minority faction was represented by one juror, and if that juror continued to refuse to change his mind after the group had directed much of their discussion at him, then he was totally excluded from the group discussion and in the end treated as an isolate.

Concluding Remarks

This chapter followed the jurors into the jury room and described how the jury discussed the trial and reached a verdict. It paid particular attention to issues which the jury has been accused of being indifferent to, ignorant of, and prejudiced against—rules of law and expert testimony. In addition it examined the social dynamics of the decision making process and showed how the jury reached consensus. The role that coalitions played in the decision making process and the importance of having at least one confederate was demonstrated in Hawkins' materials.

Strong support for the rationality of the juries' verdicts came initially from the comparison between the verdicts judges claimed they would have reached and those actually reached by real juries in the Kalven and Zeisel study. The fact that there was 80 percent overlap between the judges' and juries' decisions was enhanced by the additional information that the cases about which judges and jurors were most likely to disagree were ones that the judges felt were most evenly balanced, verdicts that in the judges' opinion could have gone either way.

Examinations of how juries treat rules of law in a variety of experimental contexts all supported the observation that juries are attentive to understanding their content and importance. On the matter of expert testimony, the Chicago studies showed the jury to be quite sophisticated in differentiating its role in the trial from that of medical experts. The jury understood the advisory capacity in which the experts' testimony was to be evaluated and showed awareness of how the experts' special knowledge and experience are likely to influence the testimony they offer.

Finally, the results reported by Hawkins and Kessler demonstrated that the sole dissenter, the minority of one, is a lonely and unattractive role that jurors like most of us in other contexts tend to avoid. If eleven jurors see eye-to-eye, it is unlikely that the twelfth will convert them or that he will withstand the pressure of holding out against a unanimous verdict. The support of only one other person makes a big difference in the jury room as it does in other social contexts. Two jurors are likely to work hard at persuading the others to their point of view, and in the end can and do hang juries.

Notes

1. Harry Kalven, Jr., and Hans Zeisel, *The American Jury* (Boston: Little, Brown, 1966).
2. Fred L. Strodtbeck and Richard Mann, "Sex Role Differentiation in Jury Deliberations," *Sociometry* 19 (March 1956): 3-11; Fred L. Strodtbeck, "Social Status in Jury Deliberations," *American Sociological Review* 22 (December 1957): 713-719; Rita J. Simon, *The Jury and the Defense of Insanity* (Boston: Little, Brown, 1967).
3. D.W. Broeder, "Plaintiff's Family Status as Affecting Juror Behavior," *Journal of Public Law* (1965).
4. Kalven and Zeisel, *The American Jury.*
5. Simon, *The Jury and the Defense of Insanity.*
6. Diane Colasanto and Joseph Sanders, "Methodological Issues in Simulated Jury Research," Unpublished ms.
7. Ibid., p. 2.
8. Ibid., p. 15-16.
9. U.S. v. Durham, 130 F Supp. 455 (1955).
10. Simon, *The Jury and the Defense of Insanity,* p. 72.
11. Ibid., p. 188.
12. A.P. Sealy and W.R. Cornish, "Juries and the Rules of Evidence," *The Criminal Law Review* (1973): 210.
13. Ibid., p. 22.
14. Rita J. Simon and Linda Mahan, "Quantifying Burdens of Proof," *Law and Society Review* (February, 1971): 322.
15. Ibid., p. 326.
16. Broeder, "Plaintiff's Family Status."
17. Simon, *The Jury and the Defense of Insanity,* p. 60.
18. Ibid., p. 61.
19. Ibid., p. 164.
20. Ibid., p. 166.
21. Ibid., p. 164.
21. Ibid., p. 164

22. Ibid.

23. Ibid., p. 93

24. Kalven and Zeisel, p. 487.

25. Ibid., p. 488.

26. Ibid., p. 489.

27. Charles Hawkins, "Interaction and Coalition Realignments in Consensus Seeking Groups: A Study of Experimental Jury Deliberations" (Ph.D. diss., University of Chicago, 1957). Reprinted with permission.

28. Ibid., p. 158.

29. Ibid., p. 130.

30. Ibid., p. 132.

31. Joan B. Kessler, "The Social Psychology of Jury Deliberations" in Rita J. Simon (ed.), *The Jury System in America.* (Beverly Hills, Calif.: Sage Publications, 1975), p. 84.

5 Jury Size and Decision Rule

David A. Vollrath and
James H. Davis

Few variables associated with small group behavior are as distinctive or easily defined as group size. Yet, almost no feature of group life has excited less theoretical concern or has received less empirical research attention. Whether this relative lack of interest has been due to the apparently mundane nature of the size issue, to a lack of theory assigning size an important conceptual role, or due to something else, the negative consequences of the oversight become evident in the face of inquiries stimulated by important practical considerations. For example, little aid was immediately available from the research literature in the face of questions raised by Supreme Court decisions affecting jury size (*Colgrove* v. *Battin,* 1973; *Williams* v. *Florida,* 1970); in particular, few small group studies, laboratory or field, addressed tasks of a complexity comparable to that of rendering a verdict.

Questions concerning decision rules or criteria for consensus on a verdict arose during approximately the same period (see *Apodaca* v. *Oregon,* 1972); *Johnson* v. *Louisiana,* 1972). The rule or procedure for aggregating votes, combining member preferences, or reaching consensus has typically been studied as a dependent variable. Thus, the social process producing a group decision or solution has been investigated as a consequence of various conditions, but rarely as a causal factor. The consequence of this tradition was a research literature almost as unhelpful as that available in connection with the group size question. Moreover, the two issues, size and decision rule, are closely related. Not only is there a policy question of how changes in both size and decision rule can affect verdicts, but there are social and political questions raised by the prospect of as few as six persons deliberating to a verdict in which only four need concur. A number of concerns, such as the need to adequately sample various subgroups throughout the community, elevate what might be a straightforward issue of procedural justice to something with larger political implications. Our attention, however, will be focused primarily on the verdict; social process, group composition, and the like, will be considered only in passing.

To begin, we review the empirical research concerning jury size and decision rule. Lamentably, these findings provide no satisfactory conclusions on the

James H. Davis is professor of psychology at the University of Illinois. David K. Vollrath is a graduate research assistant in psychology at the University of Illinois.

Preparation of this chapter was facilitated by NSF Grant BNS 77-15216, James H. Davis, Principal Investigator.

issues—a recurring problem in evaluation of proposed social change. In the face of insufficient empirical research, we suggest that theory and "thought experiments" provide valuable aid in assessing the possible effects of size and decision rule. The balance of the chapter then considers these conceptual issues.

Jury Size

Nearly a decade has passed since the U.S. Supreme Court ended the centuries-old tradition of twelve-member criminal juries (*Williams* v. *Florida,* 1970). A brief review of the research, criticism, and further Court decisions since *Williams* will highlight what we currently know and do not know about the empirical effects of jury size.

As various commentators (Saks, 1974; Zeisel, 1971) have noted, the empirical evidence cited by the Court in *Williams* amounted to a series of informal observations and assertions regarding jury sizes by members of the bench and bar, together with some misinterpreted laboratory studies of small groups. By the time the Court extended its break with tradition to civil juries (*Colgrove* v. *Battin,* 1973), a number of systematic studies (Bermant & Coppock, 1973; Institute of Judicial Administration, 1972; Kessler, 1973; Mills, 1973) had been conducted to determine the effects of jury size. These investigations were cited by the Court as convincing empirical evidence of no difference between six- and twelve-member juries. Under intense methodological scrutiny (Zeisel and Diamond, 1974), however, the studies were found to be flawed: Field investigations did not effectively rule out alternative explanations of the lack of difference; and, the single laboratory experiment used a slanted case which limited the variability possible in verdicts.

The issues involved in assessing the effects of jury size were clarified thereafter in two important commentaries. Zeisel and Diamond (1974) proposed designs for several field experiments in order to unambiguously answer the question of jury size effects. Lempert (1975), however, argued that such effects were so subtle that even these ideal experiments might fail to discern the differences.

Since *Colgrove,* another field study and a number of mock trial experiments in laboratories and courtrooms have been reported. Beiser and Varrin (1975) found that large civil juries favored the plaintiff more than small juries. Others (Grofman, 1977a; Mills, 1975; Zeisel and Diamond, 1974) have argued that these findings were due instead to the increased damages at issue and the complexity of cases brought before the larger juries. In a laboratory experiment, Davis, Kerr, Atkin, Holt, and Meek (1975) found no difference in the verdicts of six- and twelve-member student juries; however, their rape case favored the defendant to the extent that no jury returned a conviction. Valenti and Downing (1975) used separate assault cases favoring either the defense or the prosecution and observed differences in verdicts. Further analysis of the data (Grofman, 1977b; Saks, 1977) revealed that random assignment of students to juries had failed to equalize predeliberation opinion. It is not clear, therefore, that the verdict differences were the result of jury size rather than unequal sentiment between the groups beforehand.

Padawer-Singer, Singer, and Singer (1977) reported fewer hung outcomes for six- than for twelve-member juries, although no differences in the rate of conviction or acquittal occurred. (This investigation appears to be the only unchallenged report of verdict differences due to jury size!) Buckout, Weg, Reilly, and Frohboese (1977) asked actual jurors to view a videotaped murder trial in a courtroom setting, as did Padawer-Singer et al., but were forced to end the study unexpectedly. The results showed no significant verdict differences between six- and twelve-person juries, but the samples were very small. In experiments involving ex-jurors and students, Saks (1977) observed no differences in verdicts as a function of jury size. Most recently, in *Ballew* v. *Georgia* (1978), the Court held five-member juries to be unconstitutional, citing among its arguments some of the above studies which had compared only six- and twelve-member juries.

This record of empirical investigations and Court decisions concerning the size of juries is disappointing in several respects. Uncontested evidence bearing on verdict differences remains sparse, consisting primarily of the recent work of Padawer-Singer et al. (1977) and Saks (1977). Moreover, even these unchallenged data do not provide a clear answer to the question of verdict differences between six- and twelve-person juries.

The large proportion of studies alleged to be flawed is disappointing as well. Methodological problems at some level can almost always be raised, especially where the investigator lacks complete control. Sampling error can mar interpretation, even with the investigator randomly assigning subjects. Rival interpretations of results arise as the intensity of an issue grows, and, judging from the bulk of critical comment produced here, jury size engages deeply held convictions. Other features of the studies, such as limited sample size or slanted case materials, were problematic primarily because jury size effects are apparently subtle.

Flaws aside for a moment, the preponderance of negative findings within the entire set of studies suggests that jury size effects are by no means "robust" phenomena, if they exist at all. On theoretical grounds, Davis, Bray, and Holt (1977) have estimated that under certain conditions verdict differences between six- and twelve-member juries amount to a *maximum* of 8 percent. From the data of Kalven and Zeisel (1966), Lempert (1975) estimated the *range* of cases which would show effects of jury size to be only 14 percent. Thus, the failure of some studies to provide evidence on the issue may have been due to the subtle nature of jury size effects.

The use of empirical data by the Court in its decisions is also somewhat disappointing. In *Williams,* the Court cited informal observations and misinterpreted small group research in support of its opinion. In *Colgrove,* it used results which were subject to alternative interpretations. In *Ballew,* the prominent role accorded empirical evidence and accompanying critical comment was contested in a concurring opinion of three Justices which rejected "numerology" and non-adversarial review of studies. Moreover, *Ballew* has drawn the line between juries of five and six using data comparing six- and twelve-member juries. Nonetheless, the *Ballew* decision represents an especially important development in the use of empirical data by the U.S. Supreme Court (Saks, 1978).

The weak *empirical* evidence of verdict differences due to jury size has not led to the conclusion that no differences exist. Rather, *theoretical* demonstrations have supported the belief of researchers and, lately, of the Court that such size effects occur. An unusually large number of formal and informal probability models of jury decision making have been developed which predict differences in verdicts as a function of jury size. These models are discussed in a later section of this chapter.

Most research on jury size has attempted to answer the question primarily by comparing verdicts, and this has been our focus in this review. Such an approach reflects the legal philosophy that the verdict of a jury properly selected and instructed should be accepted, barring extraordinary circumstances such as jury tampering. The process by which a verdict is rendered remains concertedly shrouded in secrecy. However, Saks (1977) has suggested that, in its decisions on jury size, the Supreme Court has shown considerable concern with the actual functioning of the jury, including the deliberation process. Saks' observation seems confirmed in the recent opinion of *Ballew.* Recognizing the paucity of empirical evidence involving verdicts, the Justices considered probability models and small group research to decide several issues involving both verdicts and the deliberation process.

The speed with which a jury reaches its verdict has been one of the salient process variables in the issue of jury size because savings in judicial time have been claimed as an advantage of smaller juries. The Court rejected this claim in *Ballew,* citing a field study (Pabst, 1972) in which no significant savings in time occurred when smaller juries were adopted. Results of the studies reviewed earlier are in substantial agreement, though here, as with verdict comparisons, care must be taken to avoid Type II errors.

If future concern with differences due to jury size extends beyond verdicts to the process of deliberation, then Saks' work (1977) provides an excellent model of investigation. Saks shows that by addressing *specific legal* questions the broad expanse of small group research can manageably be brought to bear. His investigation also reflects the complexity of process data and the conflicting qualities of large and small jury process.

To summarize briefly, only a few studies of jury size effects have emerged unscathed by criticism; these offer no clear answer to the question of verdict differences. To some extent, the disappointing methodological problems in the studies were unavoidable, both because the issue is controversial and because jury effects are apparently subtle. Over the course of this history, the Supreme

Court has grown increasingly sophisticated in its treatment of empirical data. The weak empirical evidence of verdict differences has been supplanted by theoretical demonstrations of jury size effects. Attention has expanded beyond verdicts to include differences in the deliberations of different-sized juries. Through focused use of small group research, future investigations may relate speed of deliberation and other process variables to the question of jury size.

Jury Decision Rule

Soon after permitting juries of less than twelve, the U.S. Supreme Court affirmed that nonunanimous juries were constitutional in state criminal (*Apodaca* v. *Oregon,* 1972) and civil (*Johnson* v. *Louisiana,* 1972) cases. The Court relied less on empirical evidence in these opinions than it had in the decisions concerning jury size. Only the proportions of hung juries occurring in unanimous and nonunanimous jurisdictions (Kalven and Zeisel, 1966) were cited, and majority and dissenting Justices disagreed over whether the difference was important. Following these Supreme Court decisions, further empirical evidence regarding decision rules has been provided by mock trial experiments.

Evidence for the effect of decision rule on verdicts of criminal juries is reasonably clear in comparisons of the traditional unanimous rule with a two-thirds majority rule. An initial lack of significant effect, reported by Davis et al. (1975), attributable to these two decision rules may have been due to the case, which apparently so favored the defendant that no jury returned a conviction. Using a more balanced version of the case, however, Davis and his colleagues (Kerr, Atkin, Stasser, Meek, Holt, and Davis, 1976) observed that unanimous juries hung more frequently than those using a two-thirds majority rule. Another study (Saks, 1977) reported a marginally significant effect of the same sort. Nemeth (1977) composed student juries which were divided 4-to-2 in opinion, and she also observed a higher rate of hung juries under the unanimous rule. A small sample of randomly composed juries which heard a variety of cases showed no significant differences, however.

In other studies of criminal juries, a more stringent five-sixths majority rule has been compared with the unanimous rule yielding further mixed evidence for rule effects. Compared to juries deliberating under a five-sixths majority rule, unanimous juries have been observed to be: marginally more likely to hang (Bray, 1974); significantly less likely to convict when given multiple conviction alternatives (Buckout et al., 1977); or, not significantly different (Padawer-Singer et al., 1977). Consistent with theoretical predictions which are discussed later and with intuition, increasingly lax decision rules have rather clear effects on verdicts.

In contrast, two mock trial experiments using civil cases have failed to find evidence for decision rule effects. The earliest investigation of decision rule

(Broeder, 1958) found that unanimous and three-fourths majority juries did not differ significantly in damages awarded. Neither were significant differences observed in negligence decisions or in damage awards between unanimous and five-sixths majority juries (Bray and Struckman-Johnson, 1977). Several explanations of the divergence between the findings for criminal and civil juries are possible. For example, both studies here used rather stringent majority rules; perhaps a lower order, such as two-thirds majority, rule would produce a noticeable difference. Alternatively, the lack of effect of decision rule on damage awards may reflect the compromises involved in arriving at a dollar amount by, say, averaging; minorities may gain concessions rather than be outvoted. Similarly, the prospect of such bargaining over damages may affect the prior decision of negligence, again minimizing the extent to which simple voting determines the outcome. Evidence of such influence in the successive guilt and sentencing decisions in a criminal rape case is reported by Davis, Holt, Spitzer, and Stasser, 1979.

For criminal juries, then, mock trial experiments confirm the dissenting Justices' concern with the Kalven and Zeisel data: Unanimous juries appear more likely to hang than nonunanimous juries. The particular nonunanimous rule (that is, the order of majority) which replaces the traditional unanimous rule affects the clarity of this evidence, moreover. No evidence has been reported of decision rule affecting negligence or damages decisions of civil juries, although fewer studies have been conducted than with criminal juries. Surprisingly, no field investigations of decision rule have been undertaken (as far as we know), in sharp contrast to jury size research. With the methodological caveats raised in jury size investigations in hand, such field studies of actual jury verdicts would likely be very valuable in extending confidence in mock trial results or pointing out qualifications to the findings.

Saks (1977) has noted that, in view of the limited empirical data concerning trial outcomes, the Supreme Court opinions considered at length the consequences of decision rule for the deliberation process. Mock trial experiments, particularly those of Nemeth (1977) and Saks (1977) have addressed some of the questions raised by the Justices. In general, the results of these studies indicate that, while verdicts may not differ, the deliberations of unanimous and nonunanimous juries proceed differently. Not surprisingly, for example, unanimous juries require more time to reach a verdict. The decision rule under which a jury deliberates also affects the rate of communication, juror recall, the frequency of expressions of (un)friendliness, disagreement and agreement, and so forth.

Interaction of Size and Decision Rule

The interrelationship of jury size and decision rule is considered in the section immediately below. Before discussing general conceptual issues, however, we might examine a specific sort of interrelation, commonly associated with experimental design. The presence or absence of an interaction between size and decision rule shows that these features combine their effects in a multiplicative or addictive way, respectively. For example, nonunanimous juries may hang less frequently than unanimous juries, and small juries less often than large ones. Is the rate at which small, nonunanimous juries hang greater than, equal to, or less than, the sum of the rates at which small juries and nonunanimous juries hang?

Such a question is a somewhat unusual empirical query, but several mock trial experiments (Buckout et al., 1977; Davis et al., 1975; Padawer-Singer et al., 1977; Saks, 1977) have been designed to address the point. No evidence of interaction between size and decision rule has been reported for jury verdicts. That is to say, there is no empirical evidence against the notion that these features combine independently of one another to affect jury decisions.

Some models of jury decision making, however, do predict the interaction of size and rule, that is, multiplicative combination of effects. Such models are discussed later. *All* models seem to suggest that decision rule makes a relatively greater difference than jury size. And, while the issue of interaction has not yet been the subject of a Supreme Court decision, certain jurisdictions use juries which combine nonunanimous rules and smaller sizes. Saks (1977) has reported data consistent with theoretical predictions of the relative impact of the two features.

Conceptual Issues

The extent of the relationship between group size and a number of other features, such as group structure, has often been overlooked in the past. It is obvious that the number of ways in which *r* people can be arranged in one- or two-way relationships increases as *r* increases, but the role of these patterns in determining performance and social relations in turn may often seem remote. A somewhat similar state of affairs prevails for social decision rule. For example, unanimity and majority rules are identical in two-person groups; or, there are no opinion divisions of *equal* subgroups possible between two decision alternatives in three-person groups. Similarly, the order of majority which is possible depends upon the size of the group. For example, a two-thirds majority is also a simple majority in a six-person jury, but a simple majority in a jury of twelve is only seven-twelfths. Observe that we are discussing logical *possibilities,* not what groups of *r* members are inclined to do in a set of circumstances.

The situation is more complicated when there are more than two alternatives, such as a jury where a "no-decision" or hung outcome is possible along with guilty and not guilty verdicts. Individual jurors are obligated to favor guilty in a criminal trial if and only if they are convinced of the position beyond a reasonable doubt (which poses a criterial problem of importance in its own right), and obligated to vote not guilty otherwise. The individual juror may experience substantial uncertainty, but indifference or an uncertain response category is not technically permissible. Thus, while jurors have two response options, there are three possible outcomes in jury decision making: guilty, not guilty, and hung. The third possibility is, in a strict sense, a failure of the decision process, whereas the other two are the legitimate decision options to be deliberated prior to a verdict. Clearly, the possible decision rules, and thus implications about the kinds and effectiveness of different decision rules, are dependent not only upon the size of the jury, but the number of decision outcomes which are possible. In general, there may be n decision alternatives defined for individuals, but n' alternatives for groups. Sometimes $n \neq n'$, such as we have conceptualized the problem for juries.

A variety of decision alternatives may be allowed in a civil trial where various amounts of money in damages could be awarded, but only three outcomes are usually though not always pertinent in a given criminal trial. We shall consider only the three-alternative case in the immediately following discussions, but later we will explore briefly some examples where $n = n' > 3$. Several combinations of group size and decision rule are displayed in table 5-1.

A decision rule is represented as a matrix which relates the jury opinion distribution to its verdict. An entry of 1 indicates the opinion array of that row has reached a group decision for the alternative represented by that column of the matrix, whereas a 0 denotes that alternative was not chosen. Four examples are given for juries of six, nine, and twelve persons. Given various circumstances many other plans might be attractive possibilities at each size. Observe that any one rule is not strictly comparable from size to size, for example the first column of matrices. Moreover, it is easy to sense that substantially more collective effort may be required to obtain unanimity in a twelve- than a six-person jury. The last column of matrices gives one something of an intuitive grasp of that issue.

Thus, we must consider both the official decision rule assigned to the group, and the actual social process producing the verdict; the two may not be identical. In fact, such things as initial unanimities are relatively uncommon, but a unanimous consensus on a verdict may be possible after deliberation—sometimes quite protracted, often surprisingly brief. We must therefore consider that an initial disparity in opinion is possible, even likely, and debate is required to establish agreement. Some rule or criterion must be formally invoked (imposed by law) as to when a member vote or preference distribution is such that a verdict has been established. Such a consensus-establishing criterion is an *assigned* decision rule. (Actually, *decision rule* is in common usage as the generic term for anything which deals with the social plan for establishing a verdict.) In practice, the rule either applies or it does not, and thus the binary entries of the matrices given in table 5-1 are a straightforward translation of verbal principles (which are often approximate and incomplete) into explicit form.

Table 5-1
Matrices Illustrating Social-Decision-Rule Possibilities for Criminal Juries of Six, Nine, and Twelve Persons

Distribution	*Outcome*											
(G,NG)	*G*	*NG*	*H*	*G*	*NG*	*H*	*G*	*NG*	*H*	*G*	*NG*	*H*
Six-person juries												
(6,0)	1	0	0	1	0	0	1	0	0	1	0	0
(5,1)	1	0	0	1	0	0	0	0	1	0	1	0
(4,2)	1	0	0	0	0	1	0	0	1	0	1	0
(3,3)	0	0	1	0	0	1	0	0	1	0	1	0
(2,4)	0	1	0	0	0	1	0	0	1	0	1	0
(1,5)	0	1	0	0	1	0	0	0	1	0	1	0
(0,6)	0	1	0	0	1	0	0	1	0	0	1	0
Nine-person juries												
(9,0)	1	0	0	1	0	0	1	0	0	1	0	0
(8,1)	1	0	0	1	0	0	0	0	1	0	1	0
(7,2)	1	0	0	0	0	1	0	0	1	0	1	0
(6,3)	1	0	0	0	0	1	0	0	1	0	1	0
(5,4)	1	0	0	0	0	1	0	0	1	0	1	0
(4,5)	0	1	0	0	0	1	0	0	1	0	1	0
(3,6)	0	1	0	0	0	1	0	0	1	0	1	0
(2,7)	0	1	0	0	0	1	0	0	1	0	1	0
(1,8)	0	1	0	0	1	0	0	0	1	0	1	0
(0,9)	0	1	0	0	1	0	0	1	0	0	1	0
Twelve-person juries												
(12,0)	1	0	0	1	0	0	1	0	0	1	0	0
(11,1)	1	0	0	1	0	0	0	0	1	0	1	0
(10,2)	1	0	0	0	0	1	0	0	1	0	1	0
(9,3)	1	0	0	0	0	1	0	0	1	0	1	0
(8,4)	1	0	0	0	0	1	0	0	1	0	1	0
(7,5)	1	0	0	0	0	1	0	0	1	0	1	0
(6,6)	0	0	1	0	0	1	0	0	1	0	1	0
(5,7)	0	1	0	0	0	1	0	0	1	0	1	0
(4,8)	0	1	0	0	0	1	0	0	1	0	1	0
(3,9)	0	1	0	0	0	1	0	0	1	0	1	0
(2,10)	0	1	0	0	0	1	0	0	1	0	1	0
(1,11)	0	1	0	0	1	0	0	0	1	0	1	0
(0,12)	0	1	0	0	1	0	0	1	0	0	1	0

For example, the matrices of the first column reflect the popular notion of a simple majority, if it exists, as establishing the verdict, and no verdict (hung) without a simple majority, if it does not. Popular prescriptions, however, rarely provide for a contingency plan when the major idea, simple majority, does not apply. For six- and twelve-person juries a hung outcome is possible, whereas a simple majority case is thus needed for juries of nine persons; such majority juries always produce a verdict. The matrices of the third column summarize a decision rule in which a verdict is established by a unanimous jury, but is hung otherwise. The final column shows similarly the decision rule for the case where a guilty verdict results from a unanimity favoring conviction, but acquittal otherwise. Many other plans, perhaps suitable for a variety of special situations, may be conveniently described by such matrices. One of the major advantages of casting the criterion for a social decision in this form is not only the convenient summary picture it consequently affords, but its potential for aiding in arriving at more complex deductions such as the consequences of alterations in size or rule. Obviously, changes in existing social institutions may produce serious and unanticipated consequences as well as the benign goals originally sought. Few social institutions can be easily or ethically manipulated after the fashion of an experiment to assess directly effects and side-effects of social change. We will return to this issue later.

The decision rules portrayed in table 5-1 do not reflect uncertainty, variability, or relative frequency of events. In other words, while adequate for summarizing the idealized notions from conventional wisdom, they are not by themselves adequate for describing the apparent course of social decision processes in juries (or for that matter other types of small groups). For one thing, it is intuitively compelling that a (4, 2) split (guilty, not guilty) of jurors in a six-person jury may not *always* lead to a conviction as the first matrix in table 5-1 requires. Rather, we might expect that the initial division (4, 2) might lead with some *probability* to a conviction, but also therefore with some probability to a not guilty verdict or even hung. A better description of the actual social decision process might therefore be what we shall call *social-decision-scheme matrices* (Davis, 1973) in which the entries are conditional probabilities, d_{ij}, the probability that the j-th outcome (guilty, not guilty, hung for juries) occurs, given the i-th initial distribution of opinion among jurors, for example, [(12, 0), (11, 1), . . . , (0, 12)]. Examples of social-decision-scheme matrices are given in table 5-2. (Those entries which are given to two decimal places as .00 or 1.00 should actually be regarded in fact as values very close but not equal to zero or one.) All possible initial distributions of opinion (sometimes called distinguishable distributions, since alternatives, but not people, are distinguishable) are given as before along the rows, and final outcomes are given along the columns.

The matrices in the first column of the table represent social decision schemes which describe a group decision process sometimes called proportionality (Davis, 1973). A verdict of guilty or not guilty is chosen with a probability which is the proportion of jurors advocating that outcome. Observe that such a decision process does not permit any hung juries. The second column of matrices translates the idea of a two-thirds majority into an explicit form, but for six- and twelve-person juries a two-thirds majority sometimes does not exist. Notice the role of group size; a two-thirds majority is also a simple majority for six persons, but not for the two larger sizes. A supplementary scheme or

Table 5–2
Examples of Possible Social-Decision-Scheme Matrices for Criminal Juries of Six, Nine, and Twelve Persons

Distribution	*Outcome*											
(G,NG)	*G*	*NG*	*H*	*G*	*NG*	*H*	*G*	*NG*	*H*	*G*	*NG*	*H*
Six-person juries												
(6,0)	1.00	.00	.00	1.00	.00	.00	1.00	.00	.00	1.00	.00	.00
(5,1)	.83	.17	.00	1.00	.00	.00	1.00	.00	.00	.93	.07	.00
(4,2)	.67	.33	.00	1.00	.00	.00	1.00	.00	.00	.84	.16	.00
(3,3)	.50	.50	.00	.50	.50	.00	.00	.00	1.00	.16	.68	.16
(2,4)	.33	.67	.00	.00	1.00	.00	.00	1.00	.00	.06	.94	.00
(1,5)	.17	.83	.00	.00	1.00	.00	.00	1.00	.00	.00	1.00	.00
(0,6)	.00	1.00	.00	.00	1.00	.00	.00	1.00	.00	.00	1.00	.00
Nine-person juries												
(9,0)	1.00	.00	.00	1.00	.00	.00	1.00	.00	.00	1.00	.00	.00
(8,1)	.89	.11	.00	1.00	.00	.00	1.00	.00	.00	.97	.03	.00
(7,2)	.78	.22	.00	1.00	.00	.00	1.00	.00	.00	.90	.10	.00
(6,3)	.67	.33	.00	1.00	.00	.00	1.00	.00	.00	.80	.15	.05
(5,4)	.56	.44	.00	.50	.50	.00	.00	.00	1.00	.70	.20	.10
(4,5)	.44	.56	.00	.50	.50	.00	.00	.00	1.00	.05	.85	.10
(3,6)	.33	.67	.00	.00	1.00	.00	.00	1.00	.00	.05	.90	.05
(2,7)	.22	.78	.00	.00	1.00	.00	.00	1.00	.00	.00	.95	.05
(1,8)	.11	.89	.00	.00	1.00	.00	.00	1.00	.00	.00	1.00	.00
(0,9)	.00	1.00	.00	.00	1.00	.00	.00	1.00	.00	.00	1.00	.00

Table 5–2 *(Continued)*

Distribution (GNG)	*Outcome*											
	G	*NG*	*H*	*G*	*NG*	*H*	*G*	*NG*	*H*	*G*	*NG*	*H*
Twelve-person juries												
(12,0)	1.00	.00	.00	1.00	.00	.00	1.00	.00	.00	1.00	.00	.00
(11,1)	.92	.08	.00	1.00	.00	.00	1.00	.00	.00	1.00	.00	.00
(10,2)	.83	.17	.00	1.00	.00	.00	1.00	.00	.00	.97	.03	.00
(9,3)	.75	.25	.00	1.00	.00	.00	1.00	.00	.00	.95	.05	.00
(8,4)	.67	.33	.00	1.00	.00	.00	1.00	.00	.00	.85	.10	.05
(7,5)	.58	.42	.00	.50	.50	.00	.00	.00	1.00	.80	.15	.05
(6,6)	.50	.50	.00	.50	.50	.00	.00	.00	1.00	.10	.70	.15
(5,7)	.42	.58	.00	.50	.50	.00	.00	.00	1.00	.00	.90	.10
(4,8)	.33	.67	.00	.00	1.00	.00	.00	1.00	.00	.00	.90	.10
(3,9)	.25	.75	.00	.00	1.00	.00	.00	1.00	.00	.00	.95	.05
(2,10)	.17	.83	.00	.00	1.00	.00	.00	1.00	.00	.00	1.00	.00
(1,11)	.08	.92	.00	.00	1.00	.00	.00	1.00	.00	.00	1.00	.00
(0,12)	.00	1.00	.00	.00	1.00	.00	.00	1.00	.00	.00	1.00	.00

subscheme is needed for those cases (3, 3) for six-person juries, and (7, 5), (6, 6), and (5, 7) for twelve-person juries; the subscheme is equiprobability, which here assigns the two subgroups advocating guilty and not guilty each a 0.50 probability of prevailing. Again, no hung juries are allowed.

The third column of social-decision-scheme matrices also assumes a two-thirds majority plan, but the subscheme now assumes a hung jury with probability near one. A hung jury thus depends upon the probability with which nonmajorities of the requisite order will occur. The final column of matrices simply illustrates the possibility of less orderly or less familiar principles, especially the occurrence of *nonsymmetric* about the main diagonal entries. As far as we know, a verdict process such as we see in the last column of table 5-2 has not been proposed as an account of jury verdicts to date. However, the observed relative frequencies of outcomes given the various initial distributions of guilt opinions have sometimes been found to differ sharply from those decision rules implied by neat principles such as a "two-thirds majority decision rule" (Davis et al., 1979; Davis, Kerr, Stasser, Meek and Holt, 1977).

"Thought Experiments"

There is a widespread and, in our view, mistaken belief that theory is primarily important for the role it plays in basic research. A contrary view is that theory is at least as useful for research with an applied aspect, whether or not that application is immediate. Blind trial and error is especially expensive when it involves social and institutional change of one sort or another. Ethical and personal costs may be exorbitant in even the seemingly minor changes involved in, for example, the procedures for administering justice. Thus, one would like to make as accurate a projection as possible, using the most plausible assumptions available about a particular procedural change (or a failure to change). The assumptions of interest to us, of course, are those involving social behavior. Both the law and its practitioners carry implicit, if not explicit, assumptions about human social behavior. While one cannot discount the set of conventions and popular wisdom accumulated over several hundred years of legal experience, not all notions are so seasoned. Moreover, the modern analysis of alternative policies and procedures may provide a different answer than favored heretofore. (See various examples of counterintuitions discussed by Davis, Spitzer, Nagao, and Stasser, 1978, concerning various group performance phenomena.)

Empirical data are an essential part of the process of constructing the projections in the way we have discussed above. However, it seems doubtful that we shall ever have enough data for all of the questions conceivably of interest to the social engineer. Theory, especially formal theory, permitting explicit projections or predictions, offers us an attractive prospect for interpolating between existing data points and extrapolating from empirical results to areas difficult to study directly. The basic idea is to set up a *Gedankenexperiment* or thought experiment, that is, "if things work in such and such a fashion, what would be the expected effects?" (See Baker 1970, for an illustration of the thought experiment in discussions about elementary physics.) The major value, of course, may come from comparing predictions from different sets of assumptions.

Examples of how thought experiments may be used to study questions about jury size and decision rule are given in the following sections. Bear in mind that substantial changes in jury size and decision rule are no longer merely prospects, but constitute institutional alterations which are already underway in many places. Preceding sections have reviewed the empirical research results available to date. We now consider some questions which go beyond the empirical record.

Jury Size

Increases in size may be expected to influence various social processes within juries, just as we may expect the size of any group to be important. Since the verdict is the jury's very reason for existence, however, we shall concentrate our attention on the relationship between size and verdict. Two particularly important issues must be considered at the outset: the initial verdict preferences of the individual jurors; and the social decision scheme aggregating or combining those preferences. For the moment, we assume a simple majority social decision scheme, if it exists, and an equally probable decision between conviction and acquittal if it does not. We shall, of course, consider alternative assumptions later. Opinions of individual jurors obviously may vary, even when they have exactly the same trial experience. Thus, we must consider the probability with which a juror favors guilty beyond a reasonable doubt, given the evidence, P_G, and not guilty, P_{NG}, otherwise. The possible (guilty, not guilty) divisions of r jurors are thus binomially distributed in the application at hand (multinomially distributed if the number of individual decision alternatives, n, is greater than 2, as might easily arise in civil trials of various sorts).[1]

Notice that the verdict by a simple majority (otherwise conviction or acquittal with equal probability) is given by the second matrix in the top row of table 5-2. Recall that a simple majority for six-person juries is also a two-thirds majority. For juries of nine and twelve, however, the two-thirds and simple majorities are not identical. Using the simple majority, otherwise equiprobability, social decision scheme, predictions were generated for various values of $0.00 \leqslant P_G \leqslant 1.00$, and results are given in figure 5-1 for juries of three, six, nine, and twelve persons. Calculations for a similar example were tabled by Walbert, 1971, and discussed by Davis, Bray, and Holt, 1977.

Several important conclusions may be drawn from the curves of figure 5-1, given the assumptions which generated them. For one thing, the difference in

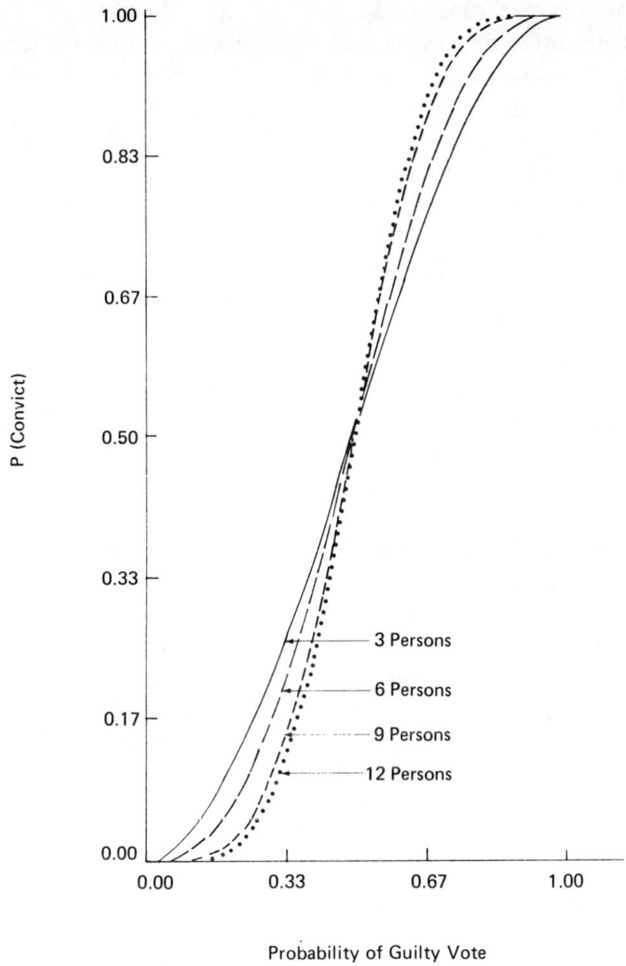

Source: From James H. Davis, Robert M. Bray, Robert W. Holt, "The Empirical Study of Decision Processes in Juries: A Critical Review," in J. Tapp and F. Levine (eds.), *Law, Justice and the Individual in Society: Psychological and Legal Issues.* Copyright © 1977 by Holt, Rinehart and Winston. Reprinted by permission of Holt, Rinehart and Winston.

Note: We assume two outcomes (guilty and not guilty), that a simple majority is needed to convict, and that ties are as likely to result in conviction as acquittal.

Figure 5-1. Probability of a Jury Conviction (P_G) as a Function of Individual Guilt Performances (P_G) for Several Different Group Sizes (r)

conviction probabilities due to different sizes is nowhere very large; that is, the difference to be expected between guilty verdicts from six- and twelve-person juries is surprisingly small in magnitude over all values of P_G, the probability of an individual juror preferring guilty. All curves converge at .00, 0.50, and 1.00, and the maximum divergences are near 0.33 and 0.67. Between juries of six and twelve, that conviction rate difference is only about 0.08. Since the bulk of the discussion has involved sizes six and twelve (Saks, 1977; *Williams* v. *Florida,* 1970; Zeisel and Diamond, 1974), a further thought experiment reported by Davis, Bray, and Holt (1977) is of particular interest at this point. Imagine that standards of statistical significance will continue as at present, namely, the Type I error rate will be set at 0.05 under the null hypothesis. With this in mind, we might ask how many subjects will be required to detect an actual difference as small as 0.08. It turns out that samples of sixty-two juries each (assuming equal size samples of six and twelve) will be needed, and thus 6(62) + 12(62) = 1116 subjects will be required. It would be a rare study indeed, whether a survey of court records or a mock (laboratory) trial, which could garner such sample sizes. One cannot easily anticipate future data sets large enough to unmask size effects, even though they may exist. Remember, the curves of figure 5-1 are not taken from data, but represent the actual state of the "world" under the terms of our theoretical assumptions.

We may summarize some of the above ideas. On the face of it, the empirical evidence scrutinized at the beginning of the chapter offered little to disconfirm the Supreme Court's arguments (*Williams* v. *Florida,* 1970) allowing a jury smaller than the traditional twelve. Yet, there is likely to be a real difference, since majority models of one sort or another are widely believed to summarize the decision outcome of deliberation. Moreover, the differences which may exist are unlikely to be detected empirically, especially as the probability of a guilty vote by the individual jurors is near .00, 1.00 or 0.50. The first two values have been mentioned by Diamond (1974) in her discussion of "slanted cases," but the similar problem of very small differences when P_G is near 0.50 is not so well known.

Finally, there is another problem which also prevents a simple answer to the deceptively simple question: "What is the best size for the jury?" Observe that the difference between any two curves in figure 5-1 *reverses direction* at P_G = 0.50. That is to say, smaller juries are *more likely* than larger juries to convict when there is a relatively small probability that individual jurors will vote for conviction, but are *less likely* to convict when jurors have a higher probability of voting for a guilty verdict. Thus, the above question may have a different answer depending upon juror sentiment at the individual level. Of course, the importance attached to the absolute magnitude of the difference due to jury size may well depend upon one's value system or the weight one gives to efficiency versus accuracy in rendering verdicts. The situation is perhaps even more subtle if we imagine that prosecution and defense attorneys are sensitive to cases in which jurors are overwhelmingly likely to favor conviction (acquittal); that is, situations in which it appears evident that P_G will be either very near 0.00 or 1.00. Such cases will probably be settled through plea bargaining. Those cases likely to yield P_G near 0.50 tend to come to trial, and differences in conviction probabilities due to size are quite small.

Verdicts with more than two outcomes. The situation is actually more complicated than indicated above—at least in the sense of a uniformly simple answer to the size question as we have posed it. We have considered juries faced with the same number of mutually exclusive and exhaustive outcomes, $n = 2$, as available to individuals. However, a jury in a civil suit might fix the size of a damage award any value within an allowable interval; a criminal jury might in effect select among several charges, as sometimes occurs when considering lesser charges in turn; and finally a jury may be unable to arrive at a verdict (hung), although indecision is not an officially defined response option. All of the foregoing imply $n > 2$, but it is the last situation (guilty, not guilty, and hung) which we wish to explore further here.

However, the social decision scheme which we have explored most thoroughly up to this point in figure 5-1 does not admit of a third alternative. Thus, we shall consider next the social decision scheme given in column three of table 5-2: A two-thirds majority, if it exists, determines the verdict with probability near one, otherwise the jury is hung with probability near one. The three outcomes (conviction, acquittal, and hung) are represented by the three different panels of figure 5-2 (adapted from Davis et al., 1975); the probability of the jury outcome is again graphed as a function of individual juror preferences for a guilty verdict.

In the first panel, we again see the reversal in the direction of the difference between juries of six and twelve, in that the probability of a conviction is *larger* given a jury of six than that from twelve, for the smaller values of P_G, but *less* than that of a jury of twelve when P_G is nearer 1.00. Unlike figure 5-2, the reversal is not symmetric; the two curves cross not at 0.50, but at 0.67 creating unequal regions of (absolute) differences around the latter value. The curves of the second panel, portraying the probability of acquittal as a function of P_G, are reflections of those in the first panel. The third panel, probability of a hung jury, shows the largest difference due to size; the twelve-person jury is much more likely to hang, in the region of $P_G = 0.50$, with only trivial reversals of this difference in both tails. Perhaps it is this latter result, likely to have been observed informally over a period of years, which fosters the attraction which smaller juries appear to possess for some. However, any enthusiasm for smaller juries should be judged against the effects to be seen in the first two panels. Given the continued and widespread acceptance of Blackstone's (1769) famous remark, "better than ten guilty persons escape than one innocent suffer," it is difficult to accept a reduction in jury size in the face of the above results.

We could discuss further a number of size issues, but we shall conclude at this point with a brief consideration of jury size and decisions with five discrete

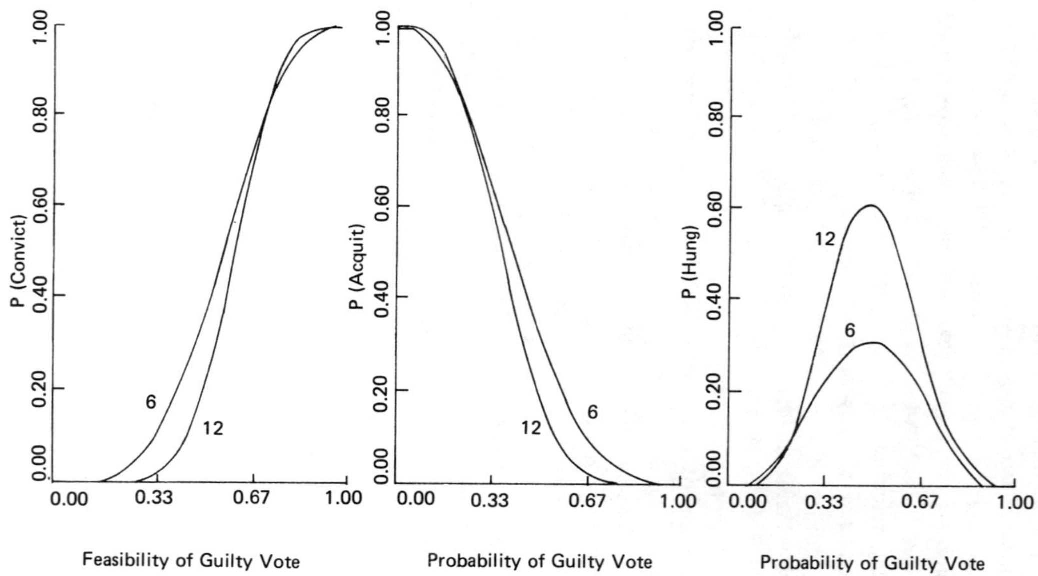

Source: From Davis, Kerr, Atkin, Holt, and Meek, 1975. Copyright American Psychological Association. Reproduced with permission.
Note: Under a two-thirds majority decision scheme for 6- and 12-person juries as a function of the probability of an individual guilty vote.

Figure 5-2. Probability of Conviction, Acquittal, and Hung Jury

verdict alternatives. Again, we must assume not only a primary social decision scheme, but adopt also a subscheme to insure that every possible opinion array which can occur is covered by some contingency plan. We have no examples with $n = 5$ displayed in table 5-2, but imagine that the jury again operates such that a simple majority determines with probability near one the alternative chosen. Otherwise an alternative is chosen with that probability which is the proportion of jury members who advocate it. Predictions from such a process are given in figure 5-3 for two cases: The left-hand panel shows a unimodal, centrally located, symmetric distribution of verdict preferences by individuals (solid curve as labeled), and the right-hand panel shows the results from a juror distribution which is positively skewed. Together, the two panels show forcefully the effects of differently distributed preferences, P_G, at the individual level. In general, ordinary majority processes, such as we have assumed here, exaggerate in the group distributions whatever perturbations exist in the individual juror distribution! (Exceptions exist when the subscheme handling the nonmajorities is contradictory in some sense to the majority scheme, and nonmajorities are quite likely to occur.)

Figure 5-3 shows the effects of size to be approximately one of *increasing* that exaggeration of perturbations which we have just noted to be characteristic of the majority process. But, note that the nine-person jury has a higher maximum than is shown for the twelve-person jury, in apparent contradiction to the idea that increasing size usually increments further the majority-exaggeration. Such irregular or disorderly progressions are not uncommon in combinatorial algebra, and often are responsible for highly counterintuitive results. Again, the effects of size are neither simple nor trivial, despite the disdain researchers have shown for its role in group performance prior to relevant Supreme Court decisions affecting juries. The effects of size as pictured in figure 5-3 may be more germane to civil than criminal juries, which have been the typical referent throughout much of this chapter.

Social Decision Rules

We mentioned earlier the close interrelationship between social decision rules and group size effects. Indeed, the immediately preceding section served as an illustration; it was not feasible to study conceptually the effects of size completely apart from social decision rule notions. We shall now focus on the question of how social decision schemes influence outcomes. To do so we regard group size as fixed and vary the social decision scheme. Assume a jury of twelve operating according to the social decision schemes: proportionality; two-thirds majority, otherwise guilty or not guilty with equiprobability; and simple majority, otherwise guilty or not guilty with equal probability. The first two social decision schemes are illustrated by the first two matrices in the last row of

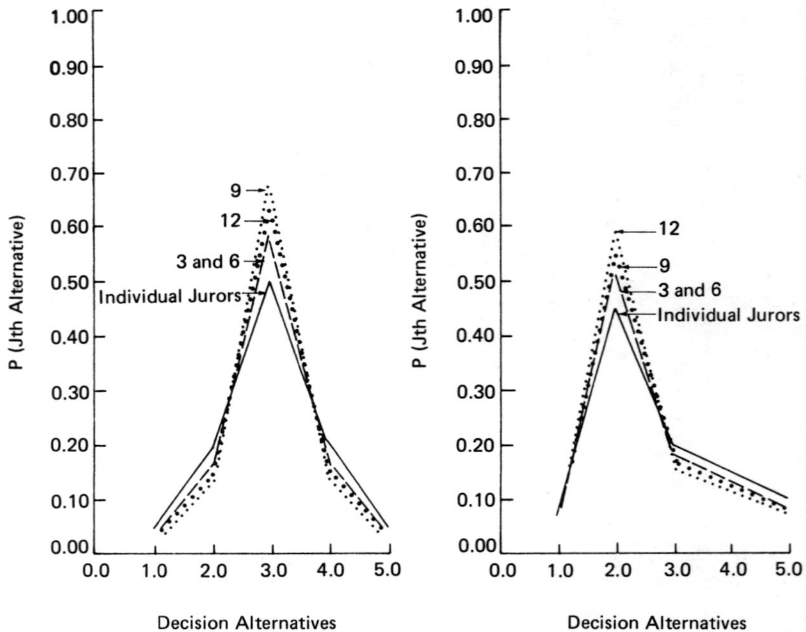

Source: James H. Davis, Robert M. Bray, Robert W. Holt, from "The Empirical Study of Decision Processes in Juries: A Critical Review," in J. Tapp and F. Levine (eds.), *Law, Justice and the Individual in Society: Psychological and Legal Issues.* Copyright © 1977 by Holt, Rinehart and Winston. Reprinted by permission of Holt, Rinehart and Winston.

Note: Each verdict alternative is chosen by individual jurors and juries of $r = 3, 6, 9$, and 12. Such scales might refer to confidence in the verdict, probability of guilt, or other responses not limited to the traditional dichotomy. The effects of individual distribution shape are illustrated by the contrast between the two subfigures.

Figure 5-3. Probability of Each Verdict Alternative

Table 5-2, and the simple majority is an obvious extension of the two-thirds majority. Observe that none of the preceding schemes allows a hung jury, and thus a single figure is sufficient to represent the nature of the group outcome.

The probability of conviction, P_G, as a function of the probability of a guilty preference by jurors is given in figure 5-4. The proportionality social decision scheme is perhaps interesting as a baseline of sorts, but the other two curves are especially notable in view of the changes in legal consensus requirements we have mentioned frequently above. Again, we see that the magnitude of the difference in conviction probabilities to be expected from decision scheme alone is small—particularly in relation to the sample sizes we typically use in empirical searches for differences of this nature. As we observed earlier, the typical study lacks sufficient statistical power to detect those differences in parameters which may actually exist, given the models' assumptions. Moreover, observe that the difference in conviction probabilities changes direction above 0.50. The two-thirds majority plan is *more* likely to result in conviction when there is a lower probability an individual juror favors guilty, than when there is a higher probability he or she will do so. Such a reversal, or interaction if you will, is not intuitively obvious from studying empirical results alone—nor is such a result evident from the store of conventional wisdom we associate with majority effects.

As before, we may go beyond the two outcomes familiar from the criminal trial and consider again the *n*-alternative case. An example using $n = 5$ alternatives is given in figure 5-5. Jury size was again fixed at twelve for all instances. The probability distribution characterizing the probability with which individual jurors preferred each decision is given by the solid line in each panel; in fact, the four panels differ only in the shape of the individual preference distribution, again illustrating the role of individual opinions in influencing the verdict distribution of juries.

The social decision schemes, the effects of which are illustrated in each panel, are generally familiar to expert and layman alike. The two-thirds majority and the simple majority models have been frequently encountered above: When an alternative possesses the requisite majority (simple in one case and two-thirds in the other), the jury chooses that alternative with probability near one. If there is no majority, an alternative is chosen with probability equal to the proportion of the jurors who advocate it. The plurality model operates in precisely the same way, except that an alternative advocated by a plurality is chosen with probability near one, otherwise proportionality. The averaging model holds that the jury will choose with probability near one that alternative (an integer) that is nearest the arithmetic average of the responses proposed. The latter model assumes at least an ordered set of alternatives; it would apply to instances such as awarding damages (amounts), but would hardly be relevant to the guilty or not guilty verdicts often arising in criminal trials. However, some type of averaging process might arise in connection with a sequence of charges ordered in severity. Such a situation has not been closely investigated to our knowledge.

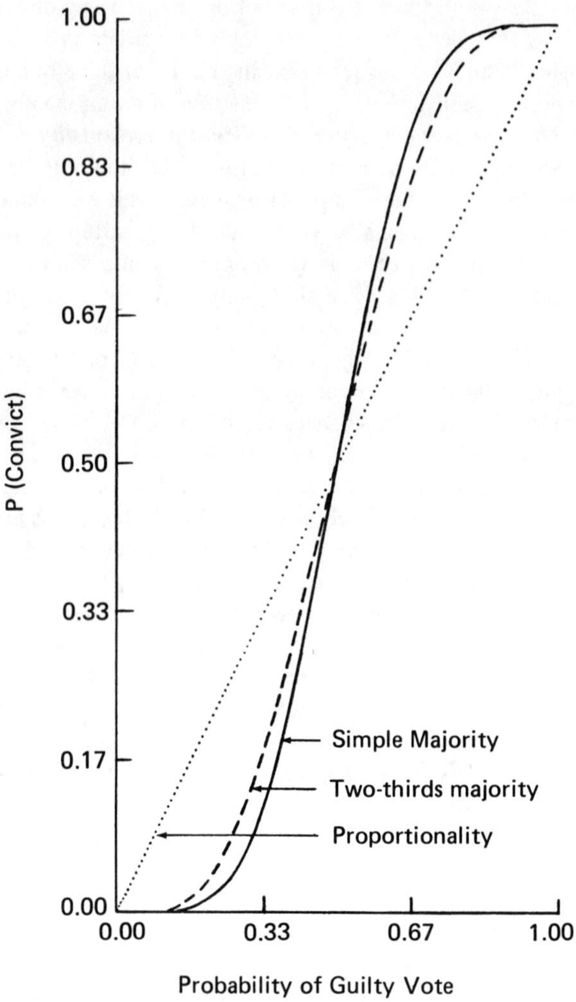

Source: From James H. Davis, Robert M. Bray, Robert W. Holt, "The Empirical Study of Decision Processes in Juries: A Critical Review," in J. Tapp and F. Levine (eds.), *Law, Justice and the Individual in Society: Psychological and Legal Issues.* Copyright © 1977 by Holt, Rinehart and Winston. Reprinted by permission of Holt, Rinehart and Winston.

Note: We assume two alternatives (guilty and not guilty) under each of the following social decision schemes: (1) *simple majority,* where a simple majority of members must favor the verdict and ties are as likely to result in conviction as acquittal; (2) *2/3 majority,* where the verdict requires 2/3 of the members in support; otherwise the probability of an alternative being chosen is the proportion of members advocating that position; (3) *proportionality,* where the probability of an alternative being selected is the proportion of members favoring that verdict.

Figure 5-4. Probability of a Conviction (P_G) in Twelve-person Juries as a Function of Individual Juror Preferences for Guilt (P_G)

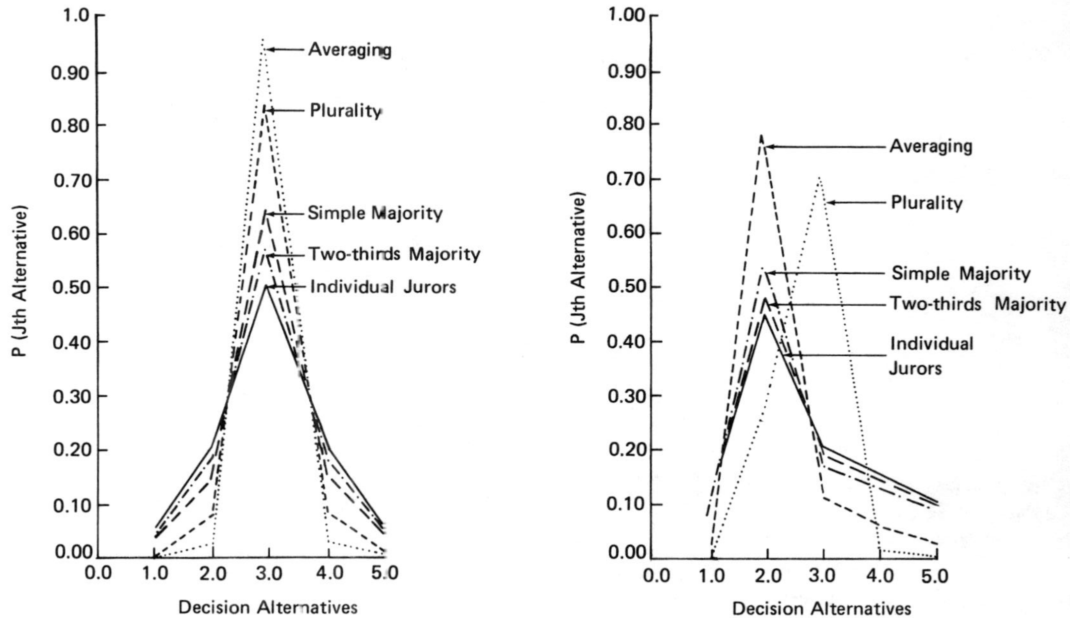

Source: James H. Davis, Robert M. Bray, Robert W. Holt, from "The Empirical Study of Decision Processes in Juries: A Critical Review," in J. Tapp and F. Levine (eds.), *Law, Justice and the Individual in Society: Psychological and Legal Issues.* Copyright © 1977 by Holt, Rinehart and Winston. Reprinted by permission of Holt, Rinehart and Winston.

Note: The individual juror preference distribution is described by the solid curve. The broken curves are probability distributions expected for 12-person juries operating on the following social decision schemes: simple majority, two-thirds majority, plurality, and averaging. The four subfigures illustrate the effects on the jury verdict distribution of changes in the form of individual juror (input) distribution, again allowing five response alternatives.

Figure 5-5. Individual Juror Preference Distributions

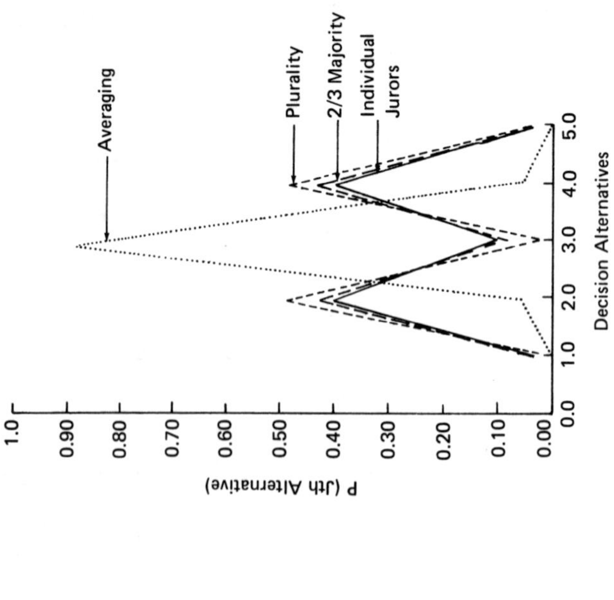

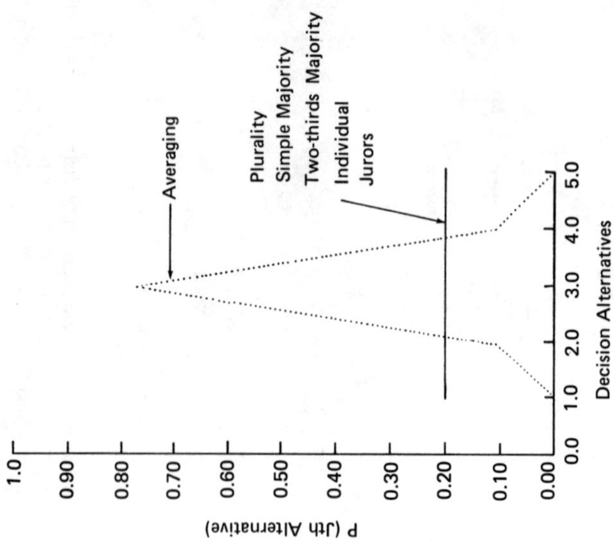

Figure 5-5. *(Continued)*

The first panel shows the effects of each of the models mentioned above when we begin with a symmetric, unimodal distribution; as we have come to expect, perturbations in the individual distribution have become more extreme in the group distributions. Due to the symmetry of the individual juror distribution, the differences among the group distributions are in magnitude not shape. One interpretation of this effect is that the weaker the consensus requirements, the more extreme the exaggeration of the vote aggregation rule! That the averaging social decision scheme is a special case is indicated by the results displayed in the second panel. Observe that we obtain the same exaggeration as displayed in the first panel, *except* the averaging model has now moved the verdict distribution toward the center of the abscissa. That is, averaging social decision scheme tends to be more moderate, that is, favors neither extreme in the face of skewed opinion distributions, and plurality-majority processes tend to exaggerate that skewness.

It is perhaps worth disgressing to note that it is this moderating or middling effect of the averaging model which conventional wisdom implies to be the typical outcome of group discussion. Thus, the choice shift (Wallach, Kogan, and Bem, 1964) phenomenon was regarded as counterintuitive relative to just such an expectation. However, averaging seems to be what researchers do to data whereas decision group members tend to act on majority principles, or perhaps plurality, as a consequence of norms requiring acquiescence to a majority, formal rules, and so on. Imagine that the abscissa represents a risk-caution continuum. Then the slightly risk-skewed individual distribution of panel two is less risky than the group decision distribution which is very skewed towards risk, whether we refer to simple or two-thirds majorities, or to plurality models. By comparing the means of such individual and group distributions we would have detected a risky shift. (Reflecting the individual distribution would, by the same argument, have produced cautious shifts.) It is tempting to explore further the "shifting" implications of plurality-majority models for juries in civil litigation. Indeed, there is a substantial literature relevant to various potential applications to juries in civil trials. However, we lack the space to consider here these ideas in detail. (See discussions by Davis, 1973; in press; Davis, Kerr, Sussmann, and Rissman, 1974.)

The third panel of figure 5-5 shows a bimodal individual distribution, and illustrates the consequences of jurors tending toward opposite extremes of response (the customary meaning of a polarized population). Each of the maxima shown for individuals will be exaggerated by plurality and majority social decision schemes used here. Thus, as a result of widely acceptable principles (a two-thirds majority) for aggregating votes, we can expect *increasing* polarization in terms of the probability distribution of jury verdicts. Averaging, on the other hand, tends to produce the middling result we noted earlier. To the extent that some sort of compromise selection of an alternative between the extremes advocated during deliberation occurs, averaging or some kind of weighted average may be an accurate representation of the outcome.

The fourth and last panel of figure 5-5 illustrates the logical consequences of input from maximally indifferent jurors. That is, the verdict preference distribution of individual jurors is uniform across all response alternatives. The result is that the plurality and majority models all predict the same thing—a uniform distribution of group verdicts. Averaging, however, has the usual effect of moving verdicts toward the middle; the group distribution under averaging will be unimodal and symmetric even given the uniform individual distribution as input.

We have in the preceding pages observed how various social decision schemes operate when several verdict alternatives are available to the jury. The four panels of figure 5-5 illustrate clearly the effects of different input (the level of the individual juror) to deliberation—and the effects on jury decisions (output) are obviously considerable. Clearly, there is a very large number of other social decision schemes which we could consider, especially for the case of $n > 2$ alternatives; the problem is compounded when one considers the many possible subschemes that might be involved. When there are several response alternatives relative to jury size, a requisite majority establishing the consensus position may be fairly improbable. In such circumstances, the subscheme may be of particular importance. We have considered only one subscheme, proportionality, but many other possibilities are doubtlessly relevant, given the variety of people, law, cases, and the like, which can arise in courtroom trials.

Discussion: Thought Experiments on Size and Decision Rule

Earlier we observed that despite the substantial affection accorded empirical research, it was by itself not enough; data alone are insufficient to answer the many questions which can and must be asked about jury behavior. We have repeatedly recommended theory guided by data, of course, as valuable for interpolating among existing data points, and for extrapolating beyond existing data sets. The need for data can be argued with equal intensity; further empirical research must guide us in selecting among the very large set of models and submodels to which our intuition and social conventions would otherwise lead us.

Additional Issues

We have repeatedly drawn attention to the commonplace observation that two jurors may not agree on a verdict preference, following a trial at which both were present. Jury composition is treated elsewhere, but we might point out here that the actual effects of different individual input, that is, persons sampled from different populations, has been illustrated in the four panels of figure 5-5. But, that discussion considered *all* jurors composing a jury as drawn from the same population—a population described perhaps by one of the probability distributions portrayed in one of the panels of figure 5-5. However, it is possible to admit mixtures to consideration—that is, the case where jurors are drawn from more than one population. In other words, more than one probability distribution must be considered as input to the social decision scheme models of the preceding sections. The actual calculations for the purpose of thought experiments can be quite tedious, but are straightforward. We will not consider these refinements in detail here (see Davis, in press; Davis et al., 1978), but we shall note that the effect of juror population mixtures (differential sampling from two or more populations) may require qualification of intuitions about size and decision rule developed from the preceding discussions. The key is the probability of sampling from the particular populations at issue.

Along these lines, it can be shown by the same strategy of thought experiments with which we are now familiar that much of the indifference currently displayed towards efforts by either defense or prosecution to obtain advantage in jury selection (Kairys, Schulman, and Harring, 1975) is misplaced. That is to say, very small advantage in the use of peremptory challenges from a knowledge of prospective jurors, not enjoyed by the other side, can result later in a substantial deformation of the verdict probability from the value it would have taken otherwise. In other words, we have seen above some unexpected effects of size and decision rule, sometimes quite small, but occasionally rather larger. But, the judgment of magnitude importance is largely relative to other considerations such as the value to be placed on making an error, and the kind of error in question (conviction of the innocent or acquittal of the guilty). A further discussion of these issues is available in Davis, in press, and Davis et al., 1978. Our major purpose for introducing these considerations at this point is to warn that previous conclusions about size and rule may require qualification in light of certain factors such as differential sampling (for whatever reason) from two or more different populations—such as a differential rate of seating defense- and prosecution-prone individuals. In general, P_G may not be constant from one population of jurors to another. Davis (in press) has observed quite different guilt preferences between males and females in each of several mock trial studies where all subjects viewed the same rape case. Similar inconstancies for P_G must be expected for other cases and other populations.

Social decision schemes, too, are not likely to be constant from population to population; variations with time and place seem very probable. If this be so, researchers cannot expect to uncover *the* social decision scheme in juries. We are, of course, referring to change in the implicit social decision scheme which is determined by social norms as well as judicial instruction. (Indeed Kerr et al., 1976, among others, have observed that mock jury verdicts are not determined exclusively by the decision rule officially assigned, at least under the conditions of their investigation.)

For example, Davis et al. (1979) have collected data from a mock (rape) trial which suggest that not only has the value of P_G increased over recent years, but the social decision scheme has likewise changed, though in fairly subtle ways. Together with other findings, these results suggest changes in social norms, at least as they pertain to verdicts in a mock trial where the crime was rape. Time-bound changes in social parameters are not surprising in a general sense, but their documentation does serve as another reminder that a single empirical result is a poor basis for social policy. In other words, there are surely temporal inconstancies to be expected in jury behavior as in other kinds of social phenomena. While not surprising on a scale of generations, substantial shifts over the course of only a few years may be somewhat more disturbing.

Of course, local trials and local jurors as well as "local law" are to some extent a tacit recognition of such variation. Unfortunately, social researchers have not always qualified their empirical reports to reflect their awareness of the fact that local norms may differ from one part of the United States to another, not to mention from country to country. We suspect that social decision scheme dependence upon culture and subculture (very probably in interaction with the type of case) may be substantial, although we currently lack data to support this suspicion.

Thought experiments of the sort we have been discussing seem well suited to the task of exploring the effects of likely cultural and temporal variations in jurors' reactions and social decision schemes or rather those social processes conveniently summarized by social decision schemes. In this way, prudent qualifications on empirical results may be conveniently formulated, and the effects of proposed changes over time and area economically assessed.

Other Models Relevant to Jury Size and Decision Rule

The review by Davis, Bray, and Holt (1977) revealed relatively more empirical study of jurors than juries, but relatively more theory available for juries than jurors. That relative difference has continued in the period since the Davis, Bray and Holt report was prepared, although both empirical and theoretical research efforts of all sorts have been intensified. We do not have the space here to explore in detail the various technical details of jury models pertinent to questions dealing with size and decision rule. (But, see Penrod and Hastie, in press, for an exhaustive review of various relevant theories.)

The Gelfand and Solomon Model. Nonetheless, we might mention in passing the work of Gelfand and Solomon as it bears on jury size and verdicts. An especially interesting feature of their work was the use of archival data from both 19th century France and 20th century United States. They extended some early work by the famous probabilist Poisson (1837) who himself had studied questions of legal procedure in much the same fashion as we have advocated above in terms of thought experiments.

Gelfand and Solomon (1974), using parameters defined by means of their model, showed that the estimated probability of a conviction (by at least a seven-twelfths majority) by French juries was quite stable from 1825 to 1830. This was a period when the assigned seven-twelfths decision rule was constant. However, the rule was changed to an eight-twelfths majority for the period 1831 to 1833; relevant calculations suggested that a similar probability for the eight-twelfths rule was smaller than that expected from the earlier results. This finding suggested that French juries did not closely obey the new prescription, a conclusion quite consistent with what we observed earlier in terms of a discrepancy between officially assigned consensus criteria and actual performance. Clearly, social norms cannot be easily overridden even by court officials. The Gelfand-Solomon result illustrates once more the importance of not only social norms and attitudes on behavior, but the necessity of including such factors when evaluating and/or engineering social change.

Other Jury Models. A number of other jury models bear in one way or another on questions of size and/or decision rule (Grofman, 1976, Nagel and Neef, 1976, Saks and Ostrom, 1975), but we shall not take the opportunity to explore them further at this time. Also, Stasser (1977), Stasser and Davis (1977), Stasser, Kerr, and Davis (in press), and especially Penrod and Hastie (1978), have explored some of the same questions, but made provision for social dynamics of interaction to operate between the initial distribution of juror opinion and the final verdict. That is to say, these authors are concerned with the nature and type of individual jurors' changes over time, and both size and decision rule are important parameters. It is as yet perhaps too early to assess the value of the dynamic models in either accounting for available empirical results or in conducting thought experiments on size and rule. The Penrod-Hastie model differs from the others mentioned above in that it is formulated as a computer program, while the other constructions are essentially mathematical models. The future is promising, however, in that few areas of social research are so well endowed with good theory.

Summary and Conclusions

The variables of group size and social decision rule had been chronically understudied when U.S. Supreme Court decisions rendered such questions of substantial practical importance. Thus, much of the research support for the discussions of this chapter has developed subsequent to these Court decisions.

Our review of research on the effects of jury size revealed very little uncontested evidence on the question, and even these data provided no clear answers. Many of the methodological shortcomings which pervade these studies are apparently due to the subtle nature of at least some jury size effects, as well as to the highly critical atmosphere in which the question has developed. Gradually, the question of jury size has been broadened from concern with verdicts to interest in differences in the process of jury deliberation as well. The focal issue has also been expanded from an empirical inquiry to include theoretical demonstrations.

Following the Supreme Court decisions allowing nonunanimous juries, numerous mock trial experiments found evidence that such juries were less likely to hang than those deliberating under a traditional unanimity rule when hearing a criminal case. The lack of effect due to decision rule on the negligence and award decisions of civil juries may reflect the compromise involved in agreeing on an amount of damages. A few studies which varied both size and decision rule observed no significant interaction between the two variables. Various predictions from the many models of jury decision making now available suggest that the effects of decision rule are larger than those of jury size, though neither tends to be very powerful.

Conceptually, size and rule are interrelated, not only with one another but with the probability of an individual voting for conviction or acquittal, the number of alternatives, and the nature of the case. We introduced the idea of a thought experiment to argue that theory has a necessary role in applied problems. While empirical data are also necessary to develop and select among theories, they are not sufficient to meet the demands of policy problems for several reasons. Even the most thorough data gathering yields a finite empirical record requiring considerable interpolation and extrapolation in view of the numerous questions arising from daily practice. The *Ballew* v. *Georgia* decision is a case in point. All available evidence had compared six- and twelve-member juries, but the question before the Court was whether five-member juries were constitutional. Empirical data which are limited by particular populations or certain temporal factors may be of little value in policy decisions which are geographically or historically far-reaching. Thus, we view the appearance of numerous theoretical approaches to jury size and decision rule as an essential development.

Much of this chapter has considered factors which interrelate to make the questions of jury size and decision rule more complex than often suspected. Yet, the appearance of simplicity persists. The number of members and the required number of votes to reach a verdict are obvious features of any jury. Questions about the effects of these features are straightforward and, unfortunately, the answers to such questions are expected to be correspondingly simple. When no simple answers are found, social investigators faced with an applied policy question are often tempted to simplify the answers. A good example of such complexity, almost assuming the form of a dilemma, is the change in direction of size and decision rule effects as a function of individual juror sentiment (recall figures 5-1 and 5-4).

In more general terms, the problem involves the availability and use of information, and poses a continuing challenge. On the issue of jury size, the Supreme Court has gradually matured in its use of empirical evidence, methodological critiques, and theoretical demonstrations. Yet, not all Justices condone the use of such information, while others still tend toward selective interpretations of research as one might marshal precedent or argument.

Perhaps those who stand at the *interface* of law and the various social sciences should accept the challenge of translating relevant research and theory for the bench and bar and, in turn, of guiding future social research to significant legal questions. Whatever the fate of the jury at the hands of Congress, legislatures, and the Court, the affection of the American public for this institution seems likely to endure.

Note

1. More specifically, the probability of each initial distribution of opinion,

$$\pi_i = \begin{bmatrix} r \\ r_G, r_{NG} \end{bmatrix} P_G^{\,r_G} P_{NG}^{\,r_{NG}}, \; i = 1, 2, \ldots, m = \begin{bmatrix} n + r - 1 \\ r \end{bmatrix},$$

may be cast as the m-tuple, $\pi = (\pi_1, \pi_2, \ldots, \pi_m)$. The jury verdict distribution, P, is then given by $\pi D = P$, where $P = (P_G, P_{NG}, P_H)$, or $P = (P_G, P_{NG})$ if hung juries are not permitted, and D is the social decision scheme matrix as illustrated in table 5-2. See Davis (1973), Davis (in press), and Stasser, Kerr, and Davis (in press) for a more comprehensive discussion of social decision scheme theory.

References

Apodaca et al. v. Oregon. 406 United States Supreme Court Reports (1972), 404–415.

Baker, A. 1970. *Modern Physics and Anti-Physics.* Reading, Mass.: Addison-Wesley.

Ballew v. Georgia. *The United States Law Week* 46, (1978): 4217–4224.

Beiser, E.N., and Varrin, R. "Six-Member Juries in the Federal Courts," *Judicature* 58, (1975): 423–433.

Bermant, G., and Coppock, R. "Outcomes of Six- and Twelve-Member Jury Trials: An Analysis of 128 Civil Cases in the State of Washington," *Washington Law Review* 48, (1973): 593–596.

Blackstone, W. 1962. *Commentaries on the Laws of England of Public Wrongs.* Boston: Beacon Press. Originally published, 1769.

Bray, R.M. "Decision Rules, Attitude Similarity, and Jury Decision Making." Unpublished doctoral dissertation, University of Illinois, 1974.

Bray, R.M., and Struckman-Johnson, C. "Effects of Juror Population, Assigned Decision Rule and Insurance Option on Decisions of Simulated Juries." Paper presented at American Psychological Association, San Francisco, August 1977.

Broeder, D.W. "The University of Chicago Jury Project," *Nebraska Law Review* 38, (1958): 744-761.

Buckout, R.; Weg, S.; Reilly, V.; and Frohboese, R. "Jury Verdicts: Comparison of 6- and 12-Person Juries and Unanimous vs. Majority Decision Rule in a Murder Trial," *Bulletin of the Psychonomic Society* 10, (1977): 175-178.

Colgrove v. Battin. 149 *United States Supreme Court Reports,* 1973, 413.

Davis, J.H. "Group Decision and Social Interaction: A Theory of Social Decision Schemes," *Psychological Review* 80, (1973): 97-125.

_____ "Group Decision and Procedural Justice." In *Progress in Social Psychology.* Edited by M. Fishbein. Hillsdale, N.J.: Erlbaum, in press.

Davis, J.H.; Bray, R.M.; and Holt, R.W. 1977. "The Empirical Study of Decision Processes in Juries: A Critical Review." In *Law, Justice and the Individual in Society: Psychological and Legal Issues.* Edited by J. Tapp and F. Levine. New York: Holt, Rinehart and Winston.

Davis, J.H.; Holt, R.W.; Spitzer, C.E.; and Stasser, G. "Consensus Requirements, Post-Decision Expectations, and Temporal Changes in Social Parameters: An Illustration with Mock Juries." Unpublished paper, University of Illinois, 1979.

Davis, J.H.; Kerr, N.L.; Atkin, R.S.; Holt, R.; and Meek, D. "The Decision Processes of 6- and 12-Person Juries Assigned Unanimous and 2/3 Majority Rules," *Journal of Personality and Social Psychology* 32, (1975): 1-14.

Davis, J.H.; Kerr, N.L.; Stasser, G.; Meek, D.; and Holt, R. "Victim Consequences, Sentence Severity, and Decision Processes in Mock Juries," *Organizational Behavior and Human Performance* 18, (1977): 346-365.

Davis, J.H.; Kerr, N.L.; Sussmann, M.; and Rissman, A.K. "Social Decision Schemes under Risk," *Journal of Personality and Social Psychology,* 30, (1974): 248-271.

Davis, J.H.; Spitzer, C.E.; Nagao, D.; and Stasser, G. 1978. "The Nature of Bias in Social Decisions by Individuals and Groups—an Example from Mock Juries." In *Dynamics of Group Decisions.* Edited by Brandstätter; J.H. Davis; and H. Schuler. Beverly Hills, Calif.: Sage.

Diamond, S.S. "A Jury Experiment Reanalyzed," *University of Michigan Journal of Law Reform* 7, (1974): 520-532.

Gelfand, A.E., and Solomon, H. "Modeling Jury Verdicts in the American Legal System," *Journal of the American Statistical Association* 69, (1974): 32-37.

Grofman, B. 1976. Not Necessarily Twelve and Not Necessarily Unanimous. Edited by G. Bermant and N. Vidmar. *Psychology and the Law.* Lexington, Mass.: D.C. Heath.

_____. "Sloppy Sampling: A Comment on Six-Member Juries in the Federal Courts," *Social Action and the Law Newsletter* 4, (1977a): 4-5.

_____ "Differential Effects of Jury Size . . . Revisited," *Social Action and the Law Newsletter* 4, (1977b): 7-11.

Institute of Judicial Administration. *A Comparison of Six- and Twelve-Member*

Juries in New Jersey Superior and County Courts. New York: Institute of Judicial Administration, 1972.

Johnson v. *Louisiana.* 406 *United States Supreme Court Reports,* 1972, 356-403.

Kairys, D., ed.; Schulman, J.; and Harring, S., co-eds. 1975. *The Jury System: New Methods for Reducing Prejudice.* Philadelphia: Philadelphia Resistance Print Shop.

Kalven, H., Jr., and Zeisel, H. 1966. *The American Jury.* Boston: Little, Brown.

Kerr, N.L.; Atkin, R.S.; Stasser, G.; Meek, D.; Holt, R.W.; and Davis, J.H. "Guilt beyond a Reasonable Doubt: Effects of Concept Definition and Assigned Decision Rule on the Judgments of Mock Jurors," *Journal of Personality and Social Psychology* 34, (1976): 282-294.

Kessler, J.B. "An Empirical Study of Six- and Twelve-Member Jury Decision-Making Processes," *University of Michigan Journal of Law Reform* 6, (1973): 712-734.

Lempert, R.O. "Uncovering Nondiscernible Differences: Empirical Research and the Jury-Size Cases," *Michigan Law Review* 73, (1975): 643-708.

Mills, L.R. "Six-Member and Twelve-Member Juries: An Empirical Study of Trial Results," *University of Michigan Journal of Law Reform* 6, (1973): 671-711.

_____. "Letter to the editor," *Judicature* 59, (1975): 59.

Nagel, S.S., and Neef, M. "Deductive Modeling to Determine an Optimum Jury Size and Fraction Required to Convict," *Washington University Law Quarterly,* Spring (1976): 933-978.

Nemeth, C. "Interactions between Jurors as a Function of Majority vs. Unanimity Decision Rules," *Journal of Applied Social Psychology* 7, (1977): 38-56.

Pabst, W.R. "Statistical Studies on the Costs of Six-Man versus Twelve-Man Juries," *William and Mary Law Review* 14, (1972): 326-336.

Padawer-Singer, A.M.; Singer, A.N.; and Singer, R.L.J. "An Experimental Study of Twelve vs. Six Member Juries under Unanimous vs. Nonunanimous Decisions." In *Psychology in the Legal Process.* Edited by B.D. Sales. New York: Spectrum.

Penrod, S., and Hastie, R. "Models of Jury Decision-Making: A Critical Review," *Psychological Bulletin.* In press.

Penrod, S. and Hastie, R. 1978. "Computer Simulation of Jury Decision-Making." Unpublished paper. Cambridge, Mass.: Harvard University.

Poisson, S.D. 1837. *Recherches sur la probabilité des jugements en matière criminelle et en matière civile, Précedées des regles générales du calcul des probabilité.* Paris: Bachelier, Imprimeur-Libraire.

Saks, M.J. "Ignorance of Science Is No Excuse," *Trial* 10, (1974): 18.

_____. 1977. *Jury Verdicts: The Role of Group Size and Social Decision Rule.* Lexington, Mass.: Lexington Books.

_____. "Jury case: Benchmark for Behavioral Research," *APA Monitor* 1978, 9, (1978): 4.

Saks, M.J., and Ostrom, T.M. "Jury Size and Consensus Requirements: The Laws of Probability v. the Laws of the Land," *Journal of Contemporary Law* 1, (1975): 163.

Stasser, G. "A Model of Social Influence during Group Discussion: An Application with Four- and Six-person Mock Juries." Unpublished doctoral dissertation, University of Illinois, 1977.

Stasser, G., and Davis, J.H. "Opinion Change during Group Discussion," *Personality and Social Psychology Bulletin* 3, (1977): 252-256.

Stasser, G.; Kerr, N.L.; and Davis, J.H. "Group Performance and Decision Making." In *Psychology of Group Influence.* Edited by P. Paulus. Hillsdale, N.J.: Erlbaum, in press.

Valenti, A.C., and Downing, L.L. "Differential Effects of Jury Size on Verdicts following Deliberation as a Function of the Apparent Guilt of a Defendant," *Journal of Personality and Social Psychology* 32, (1975): 655-663.

Walbert, D.F. "The Effect of Jury Size on the Probability of Conviction: An Evaluation of *Williams* v. *Florida*." *Case Western Reserve Law Review* 22, (1971): 529-554.

Wallach, M.A.; Kogan, N.; and Bem, D.J. "Diffusion of Responsibility and Level of Risk Taking in Groups," *Journal of Abnormal and Social Psychology* 68, (1964): 263-274.

Williams v. *Florida. Supreme Court Reporter,* 1970, 90, 1893-1914.

Zeisel, H. ". . . and Then There Were None: The Diminution of the Federal Jury," *University of Chicago Law Review* 38, (1971): 713-715.

Zeisel, H., and Diamond, S.S. "Convincing Empirical Evidence on the Six-Member Jury," *University of Chicago Law Review* 41, (1974): 281–295.

Part III
The Jury in the Limelight: How Independent and Impartial Is It?

6 The Impact of Pretrial Publicity on the Jury

In *Nebraska Press Association* v. *Stuart,*[1] the United States Supreme Court unanimously struck down a prior restraining order prohibiting pretrial press coverage of a murder case. Although the decision was an important victory for the press, it was tailored to the facts at hand and left open the possibility that restraining orders might be entered in other cases. Chief Justice Burger wrote for the Court:

> However difficult it may be, we need not rule out the possibility of showing the kind of threat to fair trial rights that would . . . justify restraint. . . . We reaffirm that the guarantees of freedom of expression are not an absolute prohibition under all circumstances, but the barriers to prior restraint remain high and the presumption against its use continues intact . . . [In this case,] the heavy burden imposed as a condition of securing prior restraint was not met . . .[2]

Justice Brennan joined by Justices Stewart and Marshall wrote a much broader concurring opinion arguing that a prior restraint on press reports is a "constitutionally impermissible method" of affording a defendant a fair trial.[3] Justices White[4] and Stevens[5] also wrote short concurring opinions indicating that they were willing to go further than the majority had gone in protecting the press.

Much of the controversy that surrounds the free press/fair trial issue as represented by the case of the *Nebraska Press Association* stems from uncertainty about the effect of pretrial publicity in juries' verdicts. This chapter examines the Court's decision in the free press/fair trial controversy by assessing the kind and amount of influence pretrial publicity is likely to have on a defendant's right to a fair trial by a jury. Answers to this inquiry will be sought by first examining the sociopsychological literature that describes experimental and other types of research on the influence of the mass media on public attitudes and opinions, and then secondly by reporting the findings of studies on how experimental and real jurors have behaved in cases in which the free press/fair trial controversy was an important issue. Its central concern is whether jurors, that is, persons who are not trained in the law are able and willing to decide guilt or innocence solely on the basis of information heard in the courtroom, which has been sifted through the rules of evidence. Only by evaluating the willingness and ability of jurors to withstand the influence of pretrial publicity, can the wisdom and the practicality of the Court's decision in *Nebraska Press Association* be evaluated.

Influence of the Mass Media on Public Attitudes and Opinion

A considerable amount of recent research and writing has analyzed the general impact of mass communications on public opinion. On the one hand, the studies question the ability of the media to shake already held beliefs. In 1959, for example, John and Matilda Riley reviewed the research in mass communications to that time and concluded that studies measuring the effects of mass media on public attitudes and behavior "demonstrat[e] that there is no direct and simple relationship between [mass] communication and [its] effect."[6] Soon thereafter, Joseph Klapper claimed that the mass media more often reinforce existing opinions than change them, and that the media are more likely to produce modifications in beliefs than conversions.[7] Along these same lines, Bernard Berelson wrote that "[c]ommunication content is more effective in influencing opinions on peripheral issues than on crucial issues. . . . The 'relevance-quotient' or 'intensity-quotient' of the issue is inversely correlated with the capacity of the communication content to change minds."[8] Moreover, laboratory studies at the Yale Social Psychology Laboratory and the literature on perception and retention indicate that the human organism does not simply hear or see what is there; on the contrary, it perceives and recalls within the limits of the stimulus situation what it wants to perceive and recall.[9]

On the other hand, the same laboratory studies have also emphasized that certain types of people are more likely to be influenced by outside sources. Intelligence and emotional characteristics have been found to be related to persuasibility. Thus, people with low self-esteem as manifested by feelings of personal inadequacy, social inhibitions, and depressive affects are predisposed to be more readily influenced than others when exposed to any type of persuasive communication.[10] Even more generally, although people often remark that "you can't believe anything you read in the newspapers," these studies show that opinions are more apt to be accepted when they come from a credible source,[11] and others have determined that the public considers the news media to be its most reliable source of information.[12]

In addition, the psychoanalytic literature contains accounts of persons unconsciously perceiving and retaining information that affects attitudes and opinions and that may interfere with conscious efforts to learn new material.[13] Thus, prospective jurors may be unaware of the influence that prejudicial publicity is having on their attitudes toward the case. For example, when they are examined during *voir dire*, prospective jurors may answer honestly that they have formed no opinion on the matter at issue, that they will decide the case on the basis of the evidence produced in court, and that they will comply with the judge's instructions prohibiting them from reading or listening to information about the case from sources outside the courtroom. In fact, however, they may have formed unconscious opinions about the case prior to their selection as jurors, and those opinions may interfere with their listening to and evaluating the information presented in the courtroom. Although no one has offered any data to support the prevalence of unconscious learning in the context of the jury, a study discussed later in this chapter sheds some light on the relationship between the responses of potential jurors prior to trial and their subsequent behavior as jurors.

In sum, the research into the influence of the mass media on public attitudes and opinions suggests that the relationships are complex and difficult to generalize. Under some conditions, the media do appear to have a direct and immediate impact, but under many others the impact is difficult to observe because the stimulus cannot be isolated, the changed opinions or behavior cannot be observed, or unconscious factors have inhibited or repressed the behavior temporarily. The relevance of such findings to judicial decisions or public policy is therefore limited and useful only in particular contexts.

Studies that Bear Directly on the Fair Trial/Free Press Controversy

All the studies concerning the jury's performance in situations involving pretrial publicity have weaknesses. The major difficulties are as follows: 1. The subjects were not real jurors but were either students, a cross-section of adults in the community, or persons whose names were drawn from voter registration lists. 2. The stimuli did not adequately characterize real trials because the subjects were exposed to audio tapes, written statements, summaries of trials, or some combination thereof. 3. The setting in which the research was conducted was not a courtroom but a university or some other type of research laboratory. Either because of the weaknesses of the research and the resulting failure to capture successfully the realism of a trial, or because the *Nebraska Press Association* Court was unaware of such studies,[14] none of them was cited in any of the opinions. For all of their individual weaknesses, however, the studies offer some useful information about the influence that publicity is likely to have on the trial procedure and the subsequent verdict.

Studies Based on Simulated Exposure to Pretrial Publicity

In 1966, two researchers gave their subjects newspaper stories about crimes that varied as to the severity of the crime and the type of prejudicial elements involved.[15] Respondents were asked to describe the suspect in the stories they read as young-old, good-bad, guilty-innocent, dumb-smart, and honest-dishonest. The evaluations were made on a 7-point scale with an option in each case for a no opinion response. The results showed that a police report of a confession by the suspect was the single most damaging element in the stories.[16] A favorable or unfavorable statement by the district attorney or a statement about the arrest or release of the defendant was not as damaging.[17] But the control condition, a newspaper containing none of the prejudicial facts described earlier, also produced a guilty response.[18]

The more information the subjects received, the more predisposed they were to form judgments. Although only 44 percent were willing to express an opinion as to whether the defendant was good or bad, intelligent or stupid, or honest or dishonest, 57 percent were willing to judge his guilt or innocence.[19] The average guilt rating on the 7-point scale was 5.7 for the unfavorable news articles and 2.9 for the articles favorable to the defendant.[20]

In another study, 120 subjects were selected from the voter registration lists of a California congressional district and divided into eight groups of 15.[21] Each group was given a newspaper story describing the arrest of a murder suspect. The stories contained various combinations of three elements: confession, evidence, and prior criminal record. After reading the story, subjects first completed a questionnaire about the suspect's guilt or innocence and then were interviewed about how they reached that decision. News of a confession was the most prejudicial element especially in combination with a criminal record, but the authors were puzzled about the rest of their results:

> The evidence and criminal record elements, by themselves or in combination, had no effect as a predictor of belief in guilt. The researchers speculated that the confession might be perceived as a message from the suspect himself, rather than from police authorities, hence its potency. In a test for intensity of readership of the story, the subjects spontaneously recalled confession, evidence and criminal record about equally, and the experimenters concluded intensity was not a factor.[22]

In a third study, ninety-seven subjects drawn from local voter registration lists listened to a 45-minute taped and edited version of a murder trial.[23] Before listening to the trial, fifty-one subjects read three sensationally written stories that made frequent reference to the prior criminal record of one of the defendants, Kessler. The other forty-six subjects read conservatively written stories that made no reference to either defendant's criminal record. After reading the three articles, and before hearing the trial, the subjects indicated on written ballots whether they had formed an opinion as to the guilt or innocence of the two defendants and, if so, what their opinion was.[24]

Table 6-1 describes the subjects' responses to pretrial publicity. The responses indicate that people are influenced by what they read and that

Table 6-1
Verdict Distribution before the Trial by Sensational and Conservative Newspaper Reports

	Sensational			*Conservative*		
Defendants	*Guilty*	*Not Guilty*	*No Opinion*	*Guilty*	*Not Guilty*	*No Opinion*
Kessler[a]	67%	21%	12%	37%	39%	24%
Anderson	53%	33%	14%	37%	39%	24%

[a]Kessler was the defendant referred to in the sensational news stories as having a prior criminal record.

sensational news coverage has more influence than sober accounts. The subjects who read the sensational stories were more likely to believe the defendant was guilty than the subjects who read the conservative accounts. Subjects who read the conservative stories were more likely to suspend judgment than those who read sensational accounts. The subjects who read the conservative accounts did not distinguish between the two defendants and were less likely to find either of them guilty.

In the second part of the experiment the jurors listened to a recording of the trial commencing with an admonition from the presiding judge:

> Before the trial begins we ask that you lay aside any opinion that you may have formed about the case and that you listen to the testimony and to the attorneys' closing statements with an open mind. The decision that you reach should be based on the evidence presented during the trial—not on the speculation of newspapers.[25]

During the trial, defendant Kessler did not take the stand; consequently, no reference was made to his criminal record. Following the trial, the jurors were again asked to arrive at individual decisions. The results appear in table 6-2.[26]

The most striking finding was that after the jurors heard the trial, most of them changed their minds and found both defendants innocent. This was true regardless of which newspaper stories the jurors had read before the trial. On the basis of news accounts alone, 67 percent of those who had read the sensational account were persuaded that Kessler was guilty; after the trial only 25 percent voted to convict him. These jurors apparently took the judge's admonition seriously and were able both to put out of their minds the prejudicial material they had read and to reach a verdict solely on the basis of what they heard at the trial.[27]

In a fourth experiment using civil rather than criminal cases, researchers at the University of Minnesota exposed undergraduates to four trials in which prejudicial news stories about the defendant's driving record were read prior to

Table 6-2
Verdict Distribution after the Trial By Sensational and Conservative Newspaper Reports

	Sensational			*Conservative*		
Defendants	*Guilty*	*Not Guilty*	*No Opinion*	*Guilty*	*Not Guilty*	*No Opinion*
Kessler	25%	73%	2%	22%	78%	–
Anderson	25%	73%	2%	22%	78%	–

a mock trial.[28] In this study, the jurors deliberated and then reported their verdicts. There were eight juries in all, only half of whom had been exposed to the prejudicial information. The results showed no difference in the verdict patterns of the experimental and control juries. Three out of four in both categories found in favor of the defendant. In three of the four juries that had been exposed to the prejudicial information, the group discussed the information and cited the judge's instruction as grounds for not allowing it to influence their verdict.[29]

More recently, Professors Barton and Padawer-Singer conducted a study on a larger scale than any of the others reported in this chapter.[30] It also contains results that are antithetical to most of the findings of the above studies. In it jurors were called from regular jury pools and asked to participate. Each juror was given either prejudicial or nonprejudicial newspaper clippings referring to the defendant. The jurors then listened to a taped and edited version of a murder trial. When the trial was over, they retired to a juryroom for their deliberations. After the jury reached a verdict or pronounced itself deadlocked, the jurors completed questionnaires probing their reactions to the experience.[31]

Table 6-3 described the verdicts of these juries. Of the ten juries, seven were unable to reach a verdict, two resulted in guilty verdicts, and one in a verdict of not guilty. The prejudiced juries resulted in one more hung jury than did the unprejudiced juries, and the only not guilty verdict came from an unprejudiced jury, suggesting that the newspaper clippings may have had an effect on the jurors' impartiality. However, the authors were reluctant to draw any conclusions from so small a sample, indicating only that the results merited further study.[32]

Shortly thereafter, the authors took their own advice and tested another set of twenty-three juries of which ten were exposed to pretrial publicity, and thirteen were not. They also added another experimental variable to the design: Jurors in five out of the ten exposed juries went through a *voir dire* but at the time they published, the authors were not prepared to report what impact the *voir dire* had. A later report on the study, however, indicated that although the results were not conclusive, *voir dire* apparently reduced the effect of prejudicial reports and impressed upon jurors the necessity of examining all arguments heard at the trial.[33]

Table 6-3
Final Verdicts and Votes of Mineola Juries

	"Exposed" or "Prejudiced" Juries[a]		*Control or "Unprejudiced" Juries*	
	Not Guilty	*Guilty*	*Not Guilty*	*Guilty*
	0	12	12	0
	2	10	8	4
	1	11	4	8
	5	7	3	9
	5	7	0	12
Jurors (*n*)	13	47	27	33
Percentage	22	78	45	55
Verdicts[b]	0	1	1	1
Hung juries	4		3	

[a] The prejudicial clippings contained information about the criminal background of the defendant and his alleged retracted confession.

[b] Verdicts = twelve unanimous votes.

The Padawer-Singer/Barton studies offer the first and only empirical support for the conclusion that jurors allow pretrial publicity to influence their verdicts. It would be useful to see exactly how much the experience of the *voir dire* altered the figures cited in table 6-4. *Voir dire* is an important part of any jury trial, and in those cases that are viewed as sensational either because of the defendants involved or the nature of the acts with which they are charged, the *voir dire* is expected to play a crucial role.[34]

A Study Based on Exposure to Actual Pretrial Publicity

In 1970, a colleague and I surveyed community attitudes one week prior to an actual murder trial.[35] During the pretrial hearings the defense had claimed that extensive news coverage of the events leading up to the trial had so prejudiced the community that a fair trial was impossible, and that a change of venue should be granted. The survey conducted by telephone using voter registration lists sought to measure the extent to which the community had followed the events leading up to the trial, had formed opinions about the guilt or innocence of the defendant, and whether they believed that the defendant could receive a fair trial in the area.[36]

Of the 130 participants, 79 percent had heard or read about the case. Three-fourths of those with knowledge about the case remembered details about the crime. Most recalled that two men had beaten the victim with golf clubs after a fight about letting other golfers "play through" and that the defendants were

Table 6-4
Final Verdicts and Votes of Brooklyn Jurors

	"Exposed"		*"Not Exposed"*		
	Not Guilty	*Guilty*	*Not Guilty*	*Guilty*	*Undecided*
	0	12	12	0	
	0	12	12	0	
	0	12	12	0	
	12	0	9	3	
	12	0	5	4	3
	12	0	0	12	
	0	12	1	1	
	0	12	5	4	2
	0	12	0	12	
	1	11	12	0	
			10	2	
			5	7	
			12	0	
Jurors (*n*)	37	83	86	55	5
Percentage	31	69	62	35	3
Verdicts	3	6	5	2	
Hung juries	1		6		

discovered hiding in the bushes.[37] When asked to describe their feelings about the case, 65 percent of those who remembered something about the case said they favored the prosecution, 27 percent characterized themselves as indifferent, and 8 percent could not answer the question. None favored the defendants. Of those who could not supply any details, 41 percent favored the prosecution, 6 percent favored the defendants, and 53 percent were indifferent.[38]

The interviewer then asked the jurors whether it would take some evidence to change their minds about what they believed happened when the victim was attacked on the golf course and, if so, what evidence it would take. Although 69 percent of those who could supply details about the case and 65 percent of those who could not responded that some evidence would change their minds, most were unable to specify the type of evidence that would change their opinions. Those who specified the information necessary to change their views generally mentioned information about the likely mental condition of the defendants at the time of the crime or about provocation.[39]

The next three items in the survey went directly to the issue of the influence of the mass media on the jury's decision. The participants were asked three questions:

> If you were called to serve on the jury in this case, do you believe you could hear the evidence, the testimony, the attorneys' arguments and the judges' instructions, with an open mind?

If you were accused of a crime such as this, would you be willing to have your case tried by a jury in the same frame of mind as your own?

Do you believe the defendants could receive a fair trial in this community?

In response to the first question, 59 percent, of both those who could supply details and those who could not, answered that they thought they were able to serve with an open mind; 30 percent thought they could not and the other 11 percent said they did not know.[40] Fifty-five percent of those who supplied details and 65 percent of those who did not were willing to have "their case" tried by jurors in the same frame of mind as their own.[41] In response to the last item, 67 percent of those who remembered details and 76 percent of those who did not, believed that the defendants could receive a fair trial in this community.[42] One of the defense attorneys submitted the results of the survey as evidence that a change-of-venue motion was needed because his client could not receive a fair trial in the community. After admitting the survey into evidence, the judge denied the motion.[43]

A jury was selected for the trial over a two-week period, during which 118 prospective jurors were examined and challenged. During that period one defendant changed his plea to guilty. He was sentenced to thirty to sixty years in prison. The trial for the second defendant lasted two weeks. It was the county's lengthiest criminal trial to that date. The jury, which had been secluded for the duration of the trial, deliberated for nine hours and found the second defendant not guilty.[44]

This study differs from those cited earlier because it had more elements of realism. The trial, the setting, and the issues were not contrived or imposed upon a group of subjects by the researcher, and the results, therefore, may have more serious implications for public policy.[45]

Concluding Remarks

The Supreme Court's opinion in *Nebraska Press Association* v. *Stuart* made no mention of the empirical studies discussed above. Nevertheless, the opinion was consistent with the bulk of the findings of those studies in coming down strongly on the side of a free press.[46] Experiments to date indicate that for the most part juries are able and willing to put aside extraneous information and base their decisions on the evidence. The results show that when ordinary citizens become jurors, they assume a special role in which they apply different standards of proof, more vigorous reasoning, and greater detachment.

Perhaps more importantly, recent experience in actual trial situations compels the same conclusion. The facts are that, despite substantial adverse publicity, Angela Davis, John Connally, and John Mitchell[47] all were acquitted. These verdicts may be the most reliable and powerful data we have about jurors' ability to withstand pretrial publicity. They indicate that not only the media, but the bench and bar should welcome the Court's decision in *Nebraska Press Association.*

In the concluding essay of a special issue of the *Stanford Law Review* (February 1977) devoted to the Free Press/Fair Trial controversy, John Kaplan commented:

> Turning, then, from the free press side of the balance to the fair trial side, I again rely on my own experience, this time as a trial lawyer and amateur student of jury behavior. In my younger days, I tried a goodly number of jury trials, some of which were surrounded by a considerable amount of publicity, and arranged to speak to most of the jurors after each trial. I did this primarily in an effort to improve my own trial skills, but also because I was interested, as a purely academic matter, in learning how jurors reacted to various aspects of the legal proceedings and to the evidence brought before them. Although I cannot cite any controlled studies or present any sophisticated statistical analyses, my "survey" does have one important advantage over all the empirical studies on the fair trial/free press issue, including those discussed in Professor Simon's Comment: I used real jurors in a real courtroom setting.
>
> The short of my conclusions is that newspaper publicity, or any other assertions of the facts of a case made outside of court, have virtually no impact upon the jury trying the case. It is not that all jurors are without prejudice; indeed, I encountered some who were frighteningly biased and even more who seemed almost irrational in the way they processed evidence. In deciding the case before them, however, the jurors almost invariably assumed as a matter important to their status that they knew more about the facts of the case than any newspaper reporter and that their superior understanding was due to their close observation of the trial itself. Moreover, I have reason to believe that jurors, like most other Americans, mistrust the accuracy of specific statements reported in the press and have a poor memory for these things. They seem to be much more influenced by other jurors' arguments, during deliberations, and generally the debates and social pressures of deliberation determine the verdict.
>
> Of course, I cannot guarantee that this sense of responsibility and of superiority over the newspapers will hold true of every juror in every publicized case. After all, we do have a large body of psychological literature, again discussed by Professor Simon, indicating that initial impressions tend to be reinforced by ambiguous evidence and, therefore, hinting that the jurors' initial impressions that are created by the media may taint the way they view the evidence. Nonetheless, whatever the results of psychological research, it seems that the accoutrements of our legal system, including, perhaps, a minimally competent *voir dire,* are in fact enough to counter most media-induced bias.

The next chapter examines juries' verdicts in some of the major and most controversial trials of the past three decades.

Notes

1. Nebraska Press Association v. Stuart, 96 S. Ct. 2791 (1976).
2. Id. at 2808.
3. Id. at 2809 (Brennan, J., concurring).
4. Id. at 2808 (White, J., concurring).
5. Id. at 2830 (Stevens, J., concurring).
6. J.W. Riley and M.W. Riley, "Mass Communication and the Social System," in R. Merton, L. Broom, and L. Cottrell (eds.), *Sociology Today* (New York: Basic Books, 1959), pp. 537, 542.
7. Joseph Klapper, *The Effects of Mass Communication* (New York: Free Press, 1960), pp. 49-50.
8. Bernard Berelson, "Communications and Public Opinion," in W. Schramm (ed.), *Modern Society* (Urbana, Ill.: University of Illinois, 1943), pp. 167, 176-177.
9. *See generally* C. Hovland, I. Janis, and H. Kelley, Communication and Persuasion (New Haven, Conn.: Yale University Press, 1953).
10. Id. at 190. This research, of course, raises interesting questions for the attorney faced with a prospective juror who may fit such a description. The juror already may have been persuaded to an opinion unfavorable to the defendant, and for that reason the attorney may wish to challenge him. On the other hand, the attorney may be able to persuade the juror of the defendant's innocence and would prefer to confront an open but weak prejudice to a latent but deeply held one. The question, of course, is a tactical one on which many factors will impinge—the strength of the prosecution's case, the degree of publicity unfavorable to the defense, the intensity of opinions held by other members of the jury pool, and the attorney's own confidence in his assessment of the particular juror being examined.
11. See Id. at 35.
12. *See* D. Krech and R. Crutchfield, *Theory and Problems of Social Psychology* 187-88 (1948).
13. R. Crowder, *Principles of Learning and Memory* 380-81 (1976); U. Neisser, *Cognitive Psychology* 215-16 (1967).
14. *But see e.g.*, Brief for Respondent at 11, Nebraska Press Ass'n v. Stuart, 96 S. Ct. 2791 (1976), citing M.D. Tans and S.H. Chaffee, "Pretrial Publicity and Juror Prejudice, 43 Journalism Q. 647 (1966).
15. Tans and Chaffee, *supra* note 14 at 648-49. This study's subjects were members of a local PTA, students in a psychology class, and members of a steel workers' auxiliary.
16. Id. at 651-652.
17. Id. at 652.
18. Id. at 521.
19. Id. at 651.
20. Id. at 652.

21. W. Wilcox and M. McCombs, "Crime Story Elements and Fair Trial/Free Press," unpublished report summarized in Wilcox, "The Press, the Jury and the Behavioral Sciences," *Journalism Monographs* 9 (20 (1968).

22. Id. at 21.

23. R. Simon, "Murder, Juries, and the Press," *Trans-Action* 3 (40), (May-June 1966).

24. Id. at 41.

25. Id. at 41.

26. Id. at 41.

27. Id. at 42.

28. F.G. Kline and D.H. Jess, "Prejudicial Publicity: Its Effects on Law School Mock Juries," Journalism Q. 43 (1966): 113.

29. Id. at 213-216.

30. Padawer-Singer and A. Barton, "The Impact of Pretrial Publicity on Jurors' Verdicts," in *The Jury System in America, supra* note 26, at 123.

31. Id. at 125-139.

32. Id. at 136.

33. Rottenberg, "Do News Reports Bias Juries?" *Col. Journalism Rev.* 15 (May-June 1976): 16, 17.

34. *See e.g.,* Nebraska Press Ass'n v. Stuart, 96 S. Ct. 2791, 2805 (1976).

35. R. Simon and T. Eimermann, "The Jury Finds Not Guilty: Another Look at Media Influence on the Jury," *Journalism Q.* 48 (1971): 393. The trial in question was Illinois v. Harris, No. 69-1629 (Champaign County Cir. Ct. February 8, 1970).

36. Of the 170 names selected for the survey, 130 agreed to participate, twenty-nine could not be reached, four refused, and seven were disqualified by occupation. Simon and Eimermann, *supra* note 48, at 343.

37. Id. at 343-44.

38. Id. at 344.

39. Id.

40. Id.

41. Id.

42. Id.

43. Id.

44. Id.

45. The following observations made by one of the jurors who served on the trial of Black Panther leaders in New York City are appropriate in this context: "Widely publicized cases raise the question of whether it is possible to find jurors who have not been influenced toward an opinion. Nonetheless, I think this problem is often exaggerated by those who underestimate how effectively a trial can pare away the inessential elements of a case and focus on the evidence and the law—provided that fairly competent judges and attorneys are at work. In addition, although of course a juror's mere claim to being open-minded is

not enough, presumably other questions can establish the nature of his experience and temperament and perspicacity." E. Kennebeck, "From the Jury Box," in *The Jury System in America, supra* note 26, at 243.

46. The Padawer-Singer/Barton studies discussed in text accompanying notes 30-34 *supra* offer the only empirical evidence to the contrary. However, the results are not yet fully reported and may indicate that expanded *voir dire* can overcome the effects of pretrial publicity. *See* text accompanying note 33 *supra.*

47. "Mitchell's attorneys had submitted to the court a private survey by pollster Albert Sindlinger, showing that 75% of a national sampling who had heard of the Watergate cover-up considered the defendants guilty. In the District of Columbia, it appeared even worse: 84 percent thought them guilty; only 2 percent thought them innocent and the remainder were undecided. Yet both [Mitchell and Stans] were acquitted." G. Graham, "From the Press," in *The Jury System in America, supra* note 26, at 202.

7 The American Jury: Instrument of Justice or of Prejudice and Conformity?

My purpose in this chapter is to examine how well the jury performs that function for which the founders of this country had the highest expectations. In brief, it is to assess whether the jury's initial function as a bulwark against oppressive government and, in the words of Lord Devlin, "as an instrument of justice,"[1] is still being performed or whether the jury in the contemporary period primarily reflects the collective prejudice and ignorance of the national citizenry. I shall go about this task by reviewing the performance of the jury in many of the major trials that have involved questions of individual liberty, the right of dissent, and other issues surrounding First Amendment civil liberties questions that have been heard in federal and state courts throughout the United States in the past three decades beginning roughly with the end of the World War II.

As a practical matter, it will not be possible to review all the jury trials heard during this period in which such issues were considered. I would defend my selection of particular trials by the criteria of their importance as attested to by experts in the law, by the attention they have received in the media, and by the objective consequences of the verdicts.

Before proceeding, a few words about how juries' verdicts in the trials to be discussed will be interpreted. Are verdicts of acquittal, for example, always to be regarded as a sign of the jury integrity and of its effectiveness as a check against governmental oppression? Likewise, are verdicts of guilty to be viewed as instances of prejudice, corruption, and compliance with governmental power? Such simplistic interpretations would distort the usefulness and the meaningfulness of this analysis. Rather what I intend to do is examine the verdicts within the context of the nature and seriousness of the acts the defendants are accused of having committed, the socio-economic–political characteristics of the defendants, the extent and tone of the media coverage, the prevailing political mood of the country, the decisions reached by judges in bench trials of a comparable type heard during the same period, and whether the juries' verdicts were upheld on appeal.

Listed in table 7-1 are the names, not the formal names by which the cases may be identified in judicial records, but the names by which they are known in the press and by common usage. For example, the trial in New York City of the thirteen Black Panthers on grounds of conspiracy will be referred to as the Panther 13 trial and not as *The People of the State of New York* v. *Lumumba Shakur et al.*

Table 7-1
Summary of Important Political Trials from 1945 to Mid-1970s

Trial	*Verdict*	*Decision on Appeal*
Period: Late 1940s to Early 1950s		
Smith Act trials: Eugene Dennis et al.	Guilty	Upheld
Alger Hiss	1st: Hung jury 8 for conviction 4 for acquittal	
	2nd: Guilty	Upheld
Julius and Ethel Rosenberg	Guilty	Upheld
Period: Late 1960s to Early 1970s		
Angela Davis	Not Guilty	
Huey Newton	Guilty of lesser charge	Reversed
New York Panther 13	Not guilty	
Chicago 8	Guilty of lesser charge	Reversed
Harrisburg 7	Hung jury 2 for conviction 10 for acquittal No retrial	
Spock, Coffin	Guilty	Reversed
Period: Mid-1970s		
Mitchell, Stans	Not guilty	
Watergate Cover-Up Trial: Haldeman, Ehrlichman, Mitchell	Guilty	Upheld

Political Trials in the Late 1940s and Early 1950s

Like the period following the end of World War I, the era of the late 1940s and early 1950s that followed the end of World War II was marked by zeal on the part of government in seeking out those individuals and political organizations whose loyalty to the United States was doubted. As in the earlier period, concern focused primarily on the political left, on the Communist party, and on "Communist front" groups, including civil rights organizations, cultural and social movements, labor unions and other political parties (for example, the American Labor party in New York State) that had been identified as supporting the Soviet Union or leftist causes generally.

Loyalty programs and oaths were introduced at the national and state levels, at universities, among trade unions, in the mass media and entertainment fields, in the state and federal bureaucracies. The Justice Department organized and published lists of organizations believed to be disloyal and subversive; passports of prominent persons in academia, entertainment, the professions and other fields (the case of Paul Robeson stands out as one of the most notorious) were revoked. Blacklists were drawn up in the movie and television industries that effectively prevented directors, actors, and writers from finding employment.

Bills such as the Mundt-Nixon bill and the McCarran Internal Security Act were passed by the Congress requiring members of the Communist party to register with the Justice Department. Failure to do so made them liable to criminal action. Both the House and the Senate activated committees on Internal Subversion (the subcommittee headed by Joseph McCarthy, junior senator from Wisconsin, became the most famous of these) that examined the personal and political histories of thousands of American citizens.

Public opinion polls conducted during this period indicated that the activities of Senator McCarthy, the passage of the Mundt-Nixon bill, and loyalty oaths as a qualification for employment received a good deal of popular support. For example, when the public was asked during debate over the Mundt-Nixon bill whether the Congress ought to pass it, 63 percent answered yes. A year or two later when asked whether they favored registration of Communist party members, 80 percent said yes in 1949 and 67 percent said yes in 1950.[2]

On the matter of loyalty oaths, 70 percent of the public agreed with the actions of the Board of Regents of the University of California when it required all of its teachers to take an oath that they were not Communists. Concerning the activities of Senator Joseph McCarthy, in the summer of 1950, the public was asked whether it thought that Senator McCarthy's charges (that there were Communists in the State Department) were doing the country more good than harm. Among those who had an opinion (16 percent did not) or were familiar with the senator's charges (16 percent were not), 57 percent compared to 43 percent believed that Senator McCarthy's charges were doing the country more good than harm.

It is within the context of this political environment that we examine the jury's action in the major political trials of this era: the Dennis case (or the Smith Act trial), the trial of Julius and Ethel Rosenberg, and the Alger Hiss case. All three involved trial by jury. In each, the defendants were eventually found guilty (the first Hiss trial resulted in a hung jury; four jurors voted for acquittal, eight for conviction). The trial court judge in the first Hiss trial and in the Rosenberg case was Irving Kaufman, in the Dennis case, Harold Medina, and in the second Hiss trial, Henry Goddard. All three cases were upheld on appeal. The defendants in the Rosenberg case were sentenced to death and were executed on June 19, 1953. Alger Hiss was sentenced to five years in prison. The eleven defendants in the Dennis case were sentenced to five years in prison. Their lawyers were also sentenced for contempt of court.

We turn first to the Dennis case. In January 1949 the United States government brought eleven top leaders of the Communist party to trial.[3] Each of them was charged with conspiracy to teach and advocate the violent overthrow of the United States government. The trial lasted twenty weeks. The first six weeks were devoted to pretrial motions which included a challenge by the defense attorneys to the federal jury system. In essence the defense challenged the system of picking blue-ribbon juries. They charged that blue-ribbon juries were "superior" citizens chosen from such lists as college directories and the Social Register. They claimed that Jews and Negroes were systematically excluded.

When the jury was finally selected, it consisted of eleven women and one man. Three of the jurors were black and nine were white. The foreman of the jury was a black woman who earned her living as a dressmaker.

In retrospect, the behavior of the defense attorneys in the Dennis trial was similar to the behavior of the attorneys in the Chicago 8 trial. Like Kunstler et al. in the Chicago 8 trial, at the end of the Dennis trial the attorneys for the defense were also charged with contempt and sentenced by the trial judge to several months in prison. During the course of the long trial, Judge Medina also declared three of the defendants, John Gates (editor of *The Daily Worker*), Henry Winston, and Gus Hall guilty of contempt, which meant that they spent the time that they were not in the courtroom in jail, rather than being free on bail. Throughout the twenty weeks that the trial lasted, supporters of the defendants picketed the courtroom, held testimonial fund-raising dinners and organized streetcorner rallies.

Unlike the press coverage of Judge Hoffman's behavior during the Chicago 8 trial, reporters wrote admiringly of Judge Medina's demeanor on the bench. *Time* magazine described one scenario as follows:

> The judge, not the U.S. Attorney, had become their main adversary. Sometimes sallies flew so fast between judge and lawyers that the jurors swiveled their heads like a gallery at a tennis match. After only two weeks of such exchanges, the jury began to fidget wearily—but Judge Medina had been at it for nine weeks before the jury entered the box. He was growing a little tired and a little testy . . .
>
> So it went as the lawyers collecting $2,275 a week from the C.P. in fees worked to goad the judge into making a prejudicial error: it would be handy on appeal. Medina occasionally reddened with wrath as they darted in at him. Isserman with his soft way, Gladstein with his air of righteous plausibility turning to outraged innocence when the judge caught him laying a legal trap. Harry Sacher, the little man with the bull voice chivying the Court then smiling impishly, eyes cast down, while the judge mildly upgraded him. Dennis rushing in occasionally to make a choked, impassioned speech. (Dennis was acting as his own attorney.)
>
> Toward the end of the week, Judge Medina handed down a patient man's exasperated opinion: 'This is the doggonedest trial I ever saw. . . . You'll probably make a motion for a mistrial, but I'm not going to take it back.'[4]

At the end of twenty weeks both sides rested. When the judge instructed the members of the jury, he told them in essence that they had one question to decide: Did the eleven Communist leaders violate the Smith Act by conspiring to "teach the duty or necessity of overthrowing or destroying the government of the United States?" The jury began its deliberations late in the afternoon of October 13. After about six hours of deliberating the jurors were taken to a hotel for the night. They continued to deliberate the next morning for about two more hours before announcing that they had reached a verdict. The jury found each of the defendants guilty.

The trial had lasted 169 days–it was the longest, and in the words of *Newsweek*, "the dreariest and most controversial criminal trial in American legal history."[5] Each of the defendants save Thompson was sentenced to five years in prison and $10,000 in fines.[6] Medina refused the defendants' request for bail pending their appeal. The verdict was appealed to both the U.S. Court of Appeals and to the Supreme Court and upheld at each level.

The first of the two Alger Hiss trials was held in the same building and at the same time as the Dennis trial. It began on May 31, 1949. The specific charge against Alger Hiss was that he had committed perjury when he testified before the federal grand jury in 1948. If Hiss had perjured himself, then he was in fact guilty of espionage consisting of delivering secret and restricted documents of state to a foreign power while he held an important position in the State Department.[7]

Unlike the Dennis and Rosenberg trials and most of the subsequent political trials of the 1960s, the business of selecting a jury for the Hiss trial was completed quickly and without any questioning of the principles of the jury system. Within 2½ hours, forty veniremen had been called and examined. All claimed they had read about and/or heard of the case. But ten men and two women were chosen who claimed that they were without prejudice in the matter.

The trial lasted twenty-seven days. Although some seventy-five witnesses testified, one witness stood out above all others. At the beginning and end, the major question posed by the two sides was: Whom will the jury believe, Whittaker Chambers the accuser or Alger Hiss the accused? Chambers, an admitted former member of the Communist underground, accused Hiss of providing him with secret and restricted documents that Hiss had access to because of his position in the State Department. According to Chambers, Hiss acted in this fashion from 1934 to 1938, when Chambers broke with the party. Chambers testified that he had urged Hiss to do the same, but Hiss had refused. Hiss, according to Chambers, might still, up to the time of the trial, be a member of a Communist cell. At first, Alger Hiss denied knowing or having ever met Whittaker Chambers. On the witness stand, Hiss, a graduate of a prep school at Duxbury, Johns Hopkins University, and Harvard Law School, and secretary to Supreme Court Justice Oliver Wendell Holmes, testified that he was not and never had been a member of the Communist party, a fellow traveler, or a Communist sympathizer. He denied that he had ever furnished, transmitted or delivered any restricted, secret or confidential documents of the State Department of any kind, character or description whatever to Whittaker Chambers or any other unauthorized person.

Twenty-seven days later, the Court told the members of the jury that if they believed Hiss, their verdict should be not guilty. If they believed Chambers, their verdict might be guilty.

The jury deliberated nineteen hours. During that time it asked the Court for a copy of the indictment, the bill of particulars, and the exhibits. Twice it asked to have the judge's charge reread to it, and four times it informed the Court that it could not agree. In the end, it was deadlocked eight for conviction, four for acquittal.

The second trial commenced on November 17, 1949. It lasted three weeks. The two main characters performed the same roles, Chambers the accuser, Hiss the accused, but the presiding judge had been changed and some of the attorneys were new. Again, a jury was selected quickly without any basic challenge to the system. Of the eight women selected seven were housewives; of the four men, one worked in an office, one was an optician, one a plant manager, and one a retired manufacturer.

The prosecution directly met the issue of the unsavoriness of their chief witness. Chambers, they said, had had an "unguided and unfortunate boyhood." After joining the Communist party, he lied, cheated, and stole for the party. But he broke with the party and repented. He testified before the House Un-American Activities Committee out of a sense of duty. Hiss's testimony in the second trial was substantially the same as it had been in the first. The major new event in the second trial was the appearance for the defense of two "expert psychiatric witnesses" who without having examined Chambers declared him to be suffering from a psychopathic personality. They reached this opinion from having observed him in the courtroom and from having studied his writing.

The judges instructed the jury on the matter of expert testimony essentially as follows:

> . . . this testimony, like all expert testimony, was purely advisory and the jury might reject the doctors' opinions entirely if it found either that "the hypothetical situation presented to it in the question was incomplete or incorrect" or "the reasons [given in support of the opinions] unsound or not convincing;" that "the jurors had seen and heard Mr. Chambers for several days while he was on the witness stand," and it was for them to say "how much weight, if any," they would give to the testimony of the experts.[8]

The jury deliberated for almost 24 hours before it announced that it had reached a verdict. It found the defendant, Alger Hiss, guilty of perjury. The Court sentenced him to five years in the penitentiary. Hiss's appeal to the Federal Court of Appeals (2nd Circuit) was rejected. The Court (Justices Chase,

Augustus Hand, and Swan) unanimously affirmed the judgment of the district court. The U.S. Supreme Court denied Hiss's petition for further review.

The trial of Ethel and Julius Rosenberg has to be the most important case that we consider because the defendants in this case were sentenced and put to death. The trial began on March 6, 1951 before Judge Irving R. Kaufman (the judge who presided over the first of the Hiss trials). The defendants were charged with conspiracy to commit espionage by transmitting atomic secrets to agents of the Soviet Union. The trial lasted approximately one month. The jury found the defendants guilty. Judge Kaufman sentenced Ethel and Julius Rosenberg to death in the electric chair. Morton Sobell, a coconspirator, was sentenced to thirty years and David Greenglass, another coconspirator who collaborated with the prosecution, was sentenced to fifteen years.[9]

On February 25, 1952, the case was appealed to the U.S. Circuit Court of Appeals, and the convictions were affirmed. On October 13, 1952, the Supreme Court declined to review the case, with Justice Black dissenting. Between then and June 19, 1953, the date Ethel and Julius Rosenberg were executed, protest rallies were held in most countries of Western Europe, pleas for clemency were sent to the president from Pope Pius, from the president of France, from clergy, statesmen, scientists such as Albert Einstein and Harold Urey, and writers all over the world. The attorneys for the Rosenbergs introduced appeals for a new trial on grounds of newly discovered evidence and that the Atomic Energy Act of 1946 should have applied to the case. The day of the execution, protest rallies attended by thousands of persons were held in New York City and in capital cities all over the world.

How important a role did the jury play in determining the fate of Julius and Ethel Rosenberg? Had the jury not found them guilty or had the jury found them guilty of lesser acts than those for which they were charged, the trial judge would not have sentenced them to death. In the hundreds of commentaries that have been written about their trial (the Rosenberg case now ranks with Sacco and Vanzetti as being among the most controversial political trials in American history) the jury is almost forgotten. Attention focused on the trial judge and to a lesser extent on the team of prosecutors and defense attorneys. In passing the sentence that he did, Judge Kaufman became the first judge ever to sentence an American citizen to death for treason during peacetime. In explaining his reason for the death sentence, Judge Kaufman said:

> I consider your crime worse than murder. . . . I believe your conduct in putting into the hands of the Russians the A-bomb . . . has already caused, in my opinion, the Communist aggression in Korea, with the resultant casualties exceeding 50,000 and who knows but that millions more of innocent people may pay the price of your treason. Indeed, by your betrayal you undoubtedly have altered the course of history . . . we have evidence of your treachery all around us every day—for the civilian defense activities thoughout the nation are aimed at preparing us for an atom bomb attack.[10]

But what of the jury? First of all, who were the members of the jury? The jury was composed of eleven men and one woman; of eleven whites and one black. Although the trial took place in New York City where about one out of every three persons is Jewish, there were no Jews on the jury. Neither were there any laborers on the jury. Almost all the jurors were managers, entrepreneurs, accountants, or auditors (five). Some had business or other ties with government agencies.

Before the jury was selected, the Court permitted the reading aloud to the prospective jurors the names of the 105 organizations that the attorney general had deemed subversive. After the list was read, Judge Kaufman asked

> Well, now, the question is whether any juror has been a member of, contributed to or been associated with, or any member of his family, or close friend, with any of those organizations that have been just read to you.

In addition to the attorney general's list, the prosecution submitted to the jury a list of 140 publications and the defense submitted a list of fourteen, all of which the judge read to the prospective jurors and asked

> As a result of having read anything in any of these papers would you be so prejudiced that you could not render a verdict in this case based on the evidence and the evidence alone?[11]

It is impossible to know specifically how exposure to the judge's announcement homogenized the characteristics of the remaining potential jurors and to know exactly which types of jurors excluded themselves from the *voir dire*. But the fact that there were no Jews and no laborers among those finally selected suggests that there had been extensive self-selection and that the twelve persons who finally qualified to determine the guilt or innocence of Julius and Ethel Rosenberg were neither representative of the community from which they were called nor peers of the defendants.

The trial was over one month after it began. The jury deliberated for about seven hours before it announced that it had reached a verdict. The jury found the defendants guilty as charged. The judge thanked the jury (a not unusual procedure) but then announced: "Again I say a great tribute is due to the FBI and Mr. Hoover for the splendid job that they have done in this case." The jury had no say in the sentence handed down by Judge Kaufman.

The Dennis, the Hiss, and the Rosenberg trials represent the three major political trials of that era. The jury found all the defendants guilty. All the verdicts were upheld on appeal.

Politicial Trials in the Late 1960s and Early 1970s

Looking back on American society only a few years, to the latter part of the 1960s, we recall an era in which the divisiveness and bitterness between generations and between racial groups was comparable only to the class bitterness of the 1930s or the regional bitterness of the Civil War era. It was a period of the worst urban race riots in the country's history, and the most severe acts of civil disorder. The United States had been involved in unpopular wars prior to Vietnam, but no other had evoked a more violent response on the part of the young people in this country than that war did.

The lawmaking and law-enforcing agencies of the government did not respond to the disorder and violence of the late 1960s as they did to the existence of Communist-led and "infiltrated" movements of the post-World War II era. Loyalty oaths, registration of political parties, subversive lists, blacklists, all of the apparatus used by the government twenty years ago were not reinstituted, perhaps because the enemy in this period was too diffuse. The loyalty issue could not be characterized as a choice between the Soviets and the Americans. No foreign ideologies were involved. The leaders of the New Left emphasized the adjective *new* as much, or more, than they did the noun *left* in describing the objectives and goals of their movement. The blacks who organized sit-ins, who set fire to urban ghettoes, and who threw rocks at the police were 100 percent Americans.

Between 1965 and 1970 a few items concerning the right to dissent appeared on national public opinion polls. In that five-year period there was a noticeable increase in the proportion who opposed dissent. For example, when asked in 1967: "Do you think people have the right to conduct peaceful demonstrations against the war in Vietnam?"[12] Sixty-eight percent of those polled said "yes." In 1970, 25 percent said "yes."

While the government was not as active in passing laws that stigmatized dissidents and restricted their activities, it did pursue them from the streets into the courtroom. The late 1960s will be remembered as the era in which the political trial and the "movement attorney" came into their own.

There were too many political trials in the late 1960s and early 1970s, for me to describe and analyze all of them in this chapter. I think I have included the major and most representative ones.[13] The defendants in the trials selected came from every stratum in American society. Some were upper middle class, well-educated professionals, who had until their involvement in radical politics enjoyed the respect and admiration of their colleagues and a broad stratum of the American public. Some were young, long-haired, pot-smoking, college-educated persons whose vocabularies consisted primarily of four-letter words. Some were militant, tough, ghetto blacks who declared with clenched fists that their goal was political power. There were men and women who belonged to Catholic orders who declared they were still loyal to their vows but were charged with conspiracy to blow up federal buildings and kidnap Henry Kissinger. One was a black university instructor who admitted membership in the Communist party and friendship with an inmate of San Quentin.

Each of the trials lasted many weeks, each involved juries whose selection was conducted with the aid of social scientists who delved deeply into the prospective jurors' socio-economic-political status as well as their psyches. In each case, the jury was sequestered for the entire length of the trial. Each of the defendants was represented by lawyers who "designed not only to refute the charges but also to introduce political and moral issues."[14]

All the trials received extensive publicity from the mass media, and most of the media during this period, as in previous eras of political trials such as the late 1940s or the 1920s (which witnessed the Debs and Sacco-Vanzetti trials) believed the defendants were dangerous and guilty of the acts for which they were charged. Most of the media were also critical of the defendants' attire, demeanor, and behavior during the trials. The defendants' failure in many instances to exhibit proper respect for the judge and for the symbols of the state were reported in a critical vein. Barkan claims that "the Chicago Eight defense achieved world-wide publicity at the expense of antagonizing the jury."

Before commenting on each of the trials separately, I think it important to emphasize that most of the defendants were acquitted or found guilty of a lesser charge. Dr. Spock and William Sloan Coffin et al. are the conspicuous exceptions. The juries in the Angela Davis trial, the Panther 13 trial, and the Chicago Conspiracy trial all decided that the defendants were either innocent of all of the acts for which they were charged or guilty of less serious acts. The defendants' color, social status, the seriousness of the acts for which they were charged, or the style and reputation of their attorneys would not have been useful predictors of the juries' verdicts. William Kunstler received about as bad a press as any of the lawyers involved in the political trials of that period, yet his clients were acquitted or found guilty of lesser charges. The lawyers in the Spock et al. trial were more sedate, respectful, and traditional but four out of the five defendants were found guilty as charged. I turn now to an examination of the characteristics of the jurors in each of the trials to see whether a useful explanation may be derived from that source.

In the Huey Newton trial, the defendant was one of the leading figures in the Black Panther party in Oakland, California. Newton was accused of shooting and killing a policeman. Prior to the examination and selection of the jury, social scientists testified for two days claiming essentially that the selection system violated the due process section of the Fourteenth Amendment. They argued that the selection procedure (a random sample of registered voters) systematically excluded low-income groups, young people, and blacks. The judge ruled that a black defendant could receive a fair trial under the prevailing system of jury selection. The attorneys then spent two weeks selecting a jury that consisted of seven women and five men. One of the men was black. By occupation, the jury included a laboratory technician, a housewife, an engineer, a secretary, a junior executive secretary, a bookkeeper, a bologna slicer, a drugstore clerk, a machinist, a bank lending official, a bank trust official, and a landlady. The tenth juror, the bank lending official and the only black on the jury, was elected foreman. After four days of deliberating, the jury found Huey Newton guilty of voluntary manslaughter, not murder. They found him not guilty of assault with a deadly weapon. The judge sentenced Huey Newton to two to fifteen years. On May 30, 1970, the California Appeals Court reversed the decision and the government opted not to appeal their decision.

In the Panther 13 trial, which took place in New York City, the jury deliberated for 2½ hours and found all of the defendants not guilty of all fifteen of the charges, which included conspiracy, attempt to commit murder, arson, and possession of dangerous instruments and weapons. The jury profile of eleven men and one woman looked like this: a composer, a history teacher, a graduate student in political science at Columbia University, two editors from leading publishing firms, a film editor from ABC, a housing authority supervisor, a supervisor of welfare workers, a post office employee, a senior clerk of a state insurance fund, a shop teacher, and a retired longshoreman. Five of the jurors were black, one was Puerto Rican.

It is interesting to compare the composition of this New York City jury with that of the jury who heard the Rosenberg case some twenty years earlier. The Rosenbergs were Jewish and of ghetto, working-class background. There were no Jews on their jury and only one person who was employed as a laborer. In the same city two decades later a trial involving thirteen members of the Black Panthers was heard by a jury of five blacks and one Puerto Rican. After the trial, one of the lawyers, Afeni, said, "All we wanted was a jury with a conscience." A friend's wife remarked, "And you got one with soul."[15]

One of the defendants in the political trials of this era was a member of the Communist party of the United States. In addition, Angela Davis was black and a supporter of the Black Panthers. The charges against her included murder and kidnapping. In his closing argument, Leo Branton, Angela Davis's attorney, addressed the jury in these words.

> Ladies and gentlemen, before I came here, my friends told me that I could not get a fair trial for Angela Davis in this country; I could not find twelve white people who would be willing to be fair to a black woman charged with the serious crimes with which she is charged in this case. . . . Whether you want to or not, you are going to be a part of history. We on the defense are a part of history. We have labored hard and long to try to get over to you the gigantic hoax that has been committed, not only against this defendant but against the name of American justice in this country.[16]

The jury in the Angela Davis trial did indeed consist of twelve white people; seven women and five men. As was the procedure in all of the political trials of this era, the defense attorneys challenged the practice of selecting jurors from the voter registration lists. They introduced testimony that included a comparison of five high-average-income election precincts with five low-average-income precincts and showed that fifty-six prospective jurors were drawn from the high-income precincts, even though there were 2,000 more people living in the low-income precincts. Judge Arnason overruled the defense's objections and directed the attorneys to proceed with the *voir dire.* With the help of five black psychologists, Moore and Branton selected twelve jurors from among a panel of 116. The task of selecting the jury took nine days and then an additional four days to pick four alternates. The jury that tried Angela Davis consisted of a maintenance electrician who had once been a school teacher; an accountant; a sales supervisor; two housewives, one of whom had a brother who had been an inmate of San Quentin; an air traffic controller; an employee of IBM; a student; an unemployed, recently divorced woman; a medical research assistant; a retired librarian; and a collection agent.

The trial began on March 27 and ended on June 2, 1972. The jury began their deliberation on a Friday afternoon. On Sunday morning they announced that they had reached a verdict. When their verdict of not guilty was announced, it seemed to stun the courtroom. After a couple of seconds of silence, some of the spectators burst into tears, some into song, some into cheers of "Right on." The district attorney said:

> I'm shocked beyond belief by the not guilty verdicts. Apparently the jury fell for the purely emotional pitch offered by the defense. Despite what happened I'm still firmly convinced Angela Davis is as responsible for the killing of Judge Harold J. Haley and the crippling of my assistant, Gary Thomas, as Jonathan Jackson and undoubtedly more so because of her age and intelligence.[17]

Eight of the jurors showed up at a party that was taking place two hours after they had announced their verdict and at the party several of them talked about what had transpired during their deliberations. According to Major:

> . . . the elimination of the only black on the panel, a person whom several of the jurors had come to know and respect might have left them with a feeling that somehow they had been complicit in a racist act. They remembered Mrs. Hemphill's "there's been a lot of things I've had to put out of my mind," knowing that she probably would never forget the experience of having been eliminated from a jury solely because of race.[18]

Major's assessment about why the jury acquitted Angela Davis is described below:

> The combination of pre-trial publicity describing Angela as a black militant Communist gun provider, coupled with the security around the trial, predisposed the jury to be apprehensive of Angela Davis. The jury had a collective sense of unease, one which was helped along by the prosecution's constant reminder of the fate of three women hostages on August 7. As the trial proceeded much of this feeling of dread was abated as the panel had an opportunity to see Angela Davis in action. Many of them were present when Angela conducted the *voir dire* of one prospective juror which resulted in his disqualification for being prejudiced against Angela for being a Communist. They were impressed by her opening statement, but more important, they observed her day after day, taking notes, conferring with her attorneys, and acting like any defendant concerned with the problem of confronting a number of serious charges.[19]

The biggest and most sensational of the political trials of this period was the Chicago Conspiracy trial. Eight defendants were charged with conspiracy to cross state lines with intent to cause a riot, to interfere with law enforcement officers and firemen in the performance of their duties, and to teach and demonstrate the use of incendiary devices. Twelve alleged coconspirators were also named but not indicted. Weiner and Froines were charged with teaching and demonstrating the use of incendiary devices, and the remaining defendants were charged with violating the Rap Brown Law: crossing state lines with intent to cause a riot. Except for Weiner and Froines, the defendants were well known.[20] The defendants included leaders of the Yippies (Abbie Mann and Jerry Rubin), a former head of Students for a Democratic Society (Tom Hayden), one of the founders and leaders of the Black Panthers (Bobby Seale), a founder of the National Mobilization Committee to End the War in Vietnam and disciple of the late A.J. Muste (David Dellinger). Judge Julius Hoffman presided. William Kunstler headed a team of defense attorneys and Thomas Foran was the chief prosecutor. The trial lasted five months. During it one of the defendants, Bobby Seale, sat in the courtroom bound and gagged. All the defendants engaged in catcalls and heckling. They refused to stand when the judge entered the courtroom, and they addressed him as Mr. Hoffman.

For a trial that had aroused so much interest and publicity and promised to be long and spectacular, the jury was selected in record time—less than a day. The reason for this according to Danelski is that:

> Judge Hoffman had ruled earlier that there would be no *voir dire* examination of prospective jurors, but that the defense and the government could submit questions which he would consider. He accepted a few of the government's questions but virtually none of the defendants'. Among those excluded were: "Do you believe that young men who refuse to participate in the armed forces because of their opposition to the war are cowards, slackers, or unpatriotic?" "Do you have any hostile feelings toward persons whose life styles differ from your own?"

> "Would you let your son or daughter marry a Yippie?" The one defense question accepted in substance was whether the prospective jurors had any close relatives and friends who were law enforcement officers or employees of the city, state, or federal governments.[21]

From the original panel of 300 prospective jurors, seventy excluded themselves. Of those remaining, the defense had seventeen peremptory challenges and the government six. The jury chosen consisted of ten women and two men. One of the men was an elderly car cleaner for the Chicago Transit Authority and the other was an unemployed house painter who lived on Skid Row. Both of the men were white, two of the ten women were black. Six of the women were housewives; one was a retired cook. The others worked as a customer's representative, a nurse's aide, a cashier.

According to Danelski, during the first witness's testimony something happened which affected the composition of the jury and perhaps the outcome of the case.

> The families of two of the jurors—Kristi King and Ruth Peterson—had received notes saying "You are being watched. The Black Panthers." The notes were reported to the FBI, and Judge Hoffman met with counsel in chambers to decide what should be done about the matter. Neither judge nor government counsel wanted the existence or contents of the notes made public, because the other jurors might learn of them. Kunstler informed Seale of the notes and told him that Foran and Schultz did not want the notes publicized. "Don't want publicity about it?" Seale retorted. "We's not going to send any stupid notes like that, man. Somebody's railroading us." Seale wrote a statement for the press that was given to Hayden. Later at a press conference, Hayden told reporters of the notes and said: "What we are facing here is a frame-up on trumped-up charges." He then read from Seale's statement: "There is a plot by the FBI and other lackey pig agents to tamper with the jury and then try to blame it on the Black Panther Party." When the judge heard of the press conference, he immediately ordered the jury sequestered.
>
> Judge Hoffman questioned jurors King and Peterson about the notes. Miss King was given the note and asked if she had seen it. She said she had not. He asked if any member of her family had brought it to her attention, and she again said no. He then said: "All right. Read it, Miss King, read it, please." After she read it aloud he asked whether, having read the note, she could continue to be fair and impartial in this case. She stared at Bobby Seale and, on the verge of tears, said, "No, sir." Kunstler objected to the revealing of the contents of the note to Miss King, but it was too late. She was excused as a juror, and Kay Richards, a twenty-three-year-old computer operator, took her place. Mrs. Peterson said she had seen the note but it did not affect her impartiality. She also said she had mentioned the note to her roommate, Mrs. Burns. The latter said the note would not affect her impartiality, and both women remained as jurors. The jury was complete and underwent no further changes.

> Far more was involved in this incident than the replacement of a juror. For the next four-and-a-half months the jury was to be sequestered—shut up with each other and federal marshals in hotel rooms, away from their families and loved ones. Perhaps such measures were inevitable, but they were a blow to the defense, because jurors often blame the defendants for their plight. Indeed, the jurors envied the defendants' freedom—all but Seale were out on bail during most of the trial—and at least one of them appreciated the sentiment of a sign Lee Weiner held up one day outside the courtroom as the jury boarded the bus for its hotel. It said, "Free the jury."[22]

The jury deliberated for four days. While the jury was out, Judge Hoffman adjudged the defendants and their lawyers guilty of 159 contempt citations and sentenced them to jail terms ranging from two months and eight days (Weiner) to four years and thirteen days (Kunstler).

According to postdeliberation interviews, initially eight jurors were for conviction on all counts and four were for acquittal. At one point the vote was 9 to 3 for conviction on all counts. Then one of the jurors suggested a compromise: a verdict of not guilty on the conspiracy charge and complete acquittal for Weiner and Froines. Danelski claims "that was the turning point"; on the fourth day of deliberations all of the jurors had agreed to the compromise."[23]

> After the verdict was announced and the jury discharged, some of the jurors expressed their views on the case and the defendants. Edward Kratzke, the jury foreman, said: "I was a streetcar conductor. I've seen guys, real bums with no soul, just a body—but when they were in front of a judge, they had their hats off. These defendants wouldn't even stand up when the judge walked in. When there's no respect, we might as well give up the United States." During a television interview Mrs. Ruth Peterson said the defendants "needed a good bath and to have their hair cut... They had no respect for nobody, not even the marshals. When they told them to get their feet off their chairs, they just put them right back again. I don't think that's nice.[24]

Each defendant received the same sentence; five years in prison and a $5,000 fine.

On May 11, 1972, a three-judge panel overturned the contempt of court conviction of Bobby Seale and defense attorneys Kunstler and Weinglass and remanded the case to the U.S. District Court for a new trial before a new judge. The judges also said that Judge Hoffman provided a caricature of judicial authority and the penalties he handed down constituted a judicial disaster. Judge Gignoux of the Federal District Court heard the trial without a jury and acquitted the defendants of 18 of the 38 contempt of court charges. Defendants Davis, Hayden, and attorney Weinglass were acquitted of all the contempt charges. The convicted defendants appealed and on November 21, 1972, the U.S. Court of Appeals for the 7th Circuit reversed the trial court. Judge Hoffman was sharply rebuked by the Appellate Court. The Court also stated that one of its reasons for reversing the trial court decision was that there had been inadequate questioning of prospective jurors about attitudes that were possibly prejudicial to the defense.

Part of the notoriety that surrounded the trial of the Harrisburg 7 was due to the fact that six of the defendants who were charged with conspiracy to raid federal offices, to bomb government property, and to kidnap the then presidential advisor, Henry Kissinger, were members of the Roman Catholic clergy.[25]

The trial was viewed by sympathizers of the defendants as an organized attack on the leadership of the Catholic Left in the United States. Lay and clerical leaders of the Catholic Left movement, liberal intellectuals, clergy of Jewish and Protestant denominations, and anti-war supporters of all denominations rallied around the Harrisburg 7. Many of them came and remained in Harrisburg for the entire length of the trial which began in January 1972 and lasted three months. They held prayer meetings and protest meetings. They called press conferences and they raised funds for the defendants' attorneys. They kept the Harrisburg 7 trial in the public eye throughout the length of the trial.

The attorneys for the defendants, which included such famous names as Ramsey Clark and Paul O'Dwyer, worked closely with a group of social scientists who aided them in selecting the jury. Throughout the *voir dire* Jay Schulman advised the defense attorneys about the prospective jurors and helped interpret and evaluate their responses. Prior to the trial, the city of Harrisburg had been surveyed and the social scientists advised the defense attorney:

> . . . on statistical grounds alone it's imperative that we fight to see as many jurors as possible. Thus if Lynch is going to reject young people, the more frames [blocks of people randomly chosen from a population] of people we go through the more likely we are to land a young person on the jury. It is also to our advantage in other ways to extend the jury selection process. The more people we see the better feel we will get for how our estimates fit the actual individuals coming through the array. A frame of 100 people: 57 will be male; 43 will be female; 8 will be under 30, 14 will be 30–39, 23 will be 40–49, 26 will be 50–59, 21 will be 60–69, 7 will be 70 and over. 33 will have less than a high school education, 46 will be high school graduates, 21 will have some college or more.[26]

> . . . In order to get twelve, close to four hundred were summoned. The panel of forty-six resulted in seventeen males, twenty-nine females. Three blacks: two female, one male. Thirty-two Protestants, five Catholics, three no-church, and six unknown. Fifteen were urban, four suburban, and twenty-seven rural and small-town. Four single women are among them and one bachelor.[27]

From this selection came twelve jurors, nine women and three men. One of the women was black, one was Catholic. One of the men was married to a Catholic. One of the women belonged to the Brethren in Christ church and had four sons, all of whom sought and received conscientious objector status. She, along with one other juror, a white Lutheran male in his forties who owned a local store, were the two holdouts for conviction. In thinking aloud about the jurors, Boudin, one of the defense attorneys, is quoted by O'Rourke as having said about that juror:

> How did he get on the jury? Boudin mused. The defense had learned he was a "staunch reform Democrat." The government had counted on getting twelve just like him. "In that crowd of forty-six [from which the twelve were picked], I said, "someone was bound to slip right past everyone; he was your Jack Ruby." Then I remembered why he did get on; he had made everyone in the courtroom laugh with his joke about golfing. The laughter bespoke a humanity that could be trusted.[28]

The jury took the case on a Thursday and eight days later on Good Friday, the day of the Crucifixion, the jury sent the judge a note, "After a long, serious, and conscientious deliberaton . . . we are unable to arrive at a unanimous verdict on nine counts of the indictment." The judge urged the jury to keep trying, citing the length of the trial and the expense involved. In the end, the jury hung 10 to 2 for acquittal on the conspiracy and threatening letter counts. They voted to convict Philip Berrigan and Sister Elizabeth McAlister on seven contraband counts.

Following the trial, two of the defendants, Fathers Wenderoth and McLaughlin, returned to their duties as diocesan priests in Baltimore. Sisters McAlister and Egan returned to New York City to continue their work with the order of the Religious of the Sacred Heart of Mary. Eqbal Ahmad went off on a vacation. Philip Berrigan was returned to Dauphin County Prison. Eventually he would be transferred back to Danbury Federal Correctional Institute.[29]

Of all the political trials of this era, none had a more illustrious roster of defendants than did the trial of the *United States of America* v. *William Sloane Coffin, Michael Ferber, Mitchell Goodman, Marcus Raskin, and Benjamin Spock.* Dr. Spock is a household word in millions of American families as the author of *The Common Sense Book of Baby and Child Care*, Marcus Raskin is the co-director of the Institute for Policy Studies in Washington, D.C., William Coffin is the chaplain at Yale University, Mitchell Goodman is a writer, and Michael Ferber was a graduate student at Harvard University. All of them were charged with carrying on a continuing conspiracy to aid, abet, and counsel violations of the Selective Service Act. Their case was tried in the Federal District Court before Judge Francis J. Ford, who at the time of trial in 1968 was 85 years old.

Judge Ford's conduct during the trial bore many similarities to that of Judge Julius Hoffman in the Chicago Conspiracy trial. Ford, like Hoffman, restricted the process of selecting the jury. Boudin, one of the lawyers for the defense, challenged the list of potential jurors on the ground that it was not representative of the community (for example, of the eighty-eight names there were only five women). Ford interrupted:

> "My understanding is that women don't have to serve unless they wish. No further colloquy from you, please." (It turned out the judge was wrong about this, he was confusing Massachusetts state courts, where women are not obliged to serve, with federal courts, in which there is no such rule.) Boudin stood his ground, announced that he intended to challenge the venire and wished to question Russell Peck, chief clerk of the court charged with assembling the jury, about his methods of selection.[30]

This was finally allowed. Peck then testified that he sent out summonses to appear for jury duty to names on the police list "which is a street list of residents." When Boudin asked Peck to demonstrate how he went about selecting the names to which he sent notices, Peck explained that

> . . . he just looked up in the air and put his finger down on the list—wherever his finger landed, he put a mark next to the name and that was the name to receive the notice. "Is there a reason why you don't use the method of taking every third, fourth, or ninth name instead of sort of looking in the air and putting your finger on the book?" asked Boudin. "I would suppose there isn't enough time and help to make the mathematical computations necessary. . ."[31]

According to Mitford, a Harvard mathematics major sitting in the audience, after a few minutes of writing in his notebook, passed a note to the press which explained in essence that if the selection had been truly random, the probability of this proportion of women to men (five out of eighty-eight) would be about one in a trillion.

James St. Clair, another of the defense attorneys, elicited from the Chief Clerk the opinion that women who show up for jury duty, particularly housewives, are more likely to be excused than men, and this makes for more paperwork. But Judge Ford had had enough. He denied Boudin's motion and insisted that the attorneys go about their business of selecting a jury. The defense was allowed fifteen peremptory challenges and the government ten. The task was completed in a day. The jury consisted of twelve white males. The two women and one black male whose names had been called were challenged by the government. Of the men, two were self-employed, six were white-collar employees, three were blue-collar workers, and one was a professional. They were meat cutters, printers, hardware clerks, loan supervisors, technicians, engineers, customer service representatives. According to Mitford, James St. Clair groaned when he saw the list and said "I wanted mothers, beards, and eggheads."[32]

The trial lasted four weeks. At the end of it, the Judge charged the jury.

> Members of the jury, our duty is joint. There are two domains in which we serve. It is your duty to receive the applicable law from me, and it is my duty to explain it to you as correctly as I can.
>
> You must apply the law that I lay down. If I fall into error in laying down the principles of law, my error or errors can be reviewed in a higher court. If you apply your own law and make an error, it cannot be reviewed and corrected.
>
> Your domain is the determination of the facts. . . .

The defense attorneys had submitted instructions bearing on the motives of the accused. For example, Boudin, on criminal intent, had written:

> It is for the jury to determine the fact as to whether the defendants acted in good or bad faith, or with an evil or innocent intent. You may take into consideration the sincerity or insincerity of the defendants' belief that the war in Vietnam was illegal and that the draft was unconstitutional. If you find that the defendants sincerely and in good faith entertained such a belief, it is your duty to acquit.

Judge Ford, however, used none of the instructions proposed by any of the defendants' attorneys. He did, however, adopt the language that the prosecuting attorney, John Wall, had used in his closing argument and instructed the jury as follows:

> Motive, no matter how laudable or praiseworthy that motive may be, cannot negate a specific intent to commit a crime. Good or innocent personal motive alone is never a defense where the act committed is an intentional violation of law—a crime. . . .
>
> When a statute has been knowingly violated, to show that a defendant had a good motive—such as dissemination of religious beliefs or the fulfilling, as he saw it, of a mission imposed upon him by the Deity, or his conscience—is no excuse whatsoever.
>
> There is no freedom to knowingly conspire to violate a law of the United States with impunity merely because one believes or doubts that the law is immoral or illegal or unconstitutional . . . a bona fide, sincere belief on the defendants' part that the Vietnam conflict and the conscription of young men to serve in it was illegal, immoral, or unconstitutional, or a belief that the Selective Service Act was unconstitutional, or a belief that they were protected by a constitutional right of free speech, would be no defense or excuse whatsoever to an intentional and wilful violation of that law by the defendants, and such beliefs, members of the jury, must not be considered by you in determining the guilt or non-guilt of the defendants.
>
> Further, I charge you that if you should find from the evidence that the

> defendants, or any of them, purposed to test the law by conspiring to counsel, aid, or abet someone to violate the law, then the fact that their purpose was to make a test case is no defense to the charge here presented against them . . . the reason for such violation is immaterial to you in your consideration of the question of their guilt or innocence.

The jury deliberated for almost 8 hours. They found all the defendants, save Raskin, guilty of all of the charges but conspiracy to turn in their draft cards.

Judge Ford's remarks before sentencing the defendants were reminiscent of those made by Judge Kaufman in the trial of Julius and Ethel Rosenberg. Kaufman held the Rosenbergs responsible for the Korean War and the death of 50,000 American soldiers. Ford said to Spock, Coffin, et al.:

> The government has charged in this case what amounts to rebellion against the law. . . . The defendants have been found guilty of intentional and willful violation of the law. . . . Rebellion against the law is in the nature of treason. The law deserves our obedience. . . .

He then sentenced the four of them to two years in prison and fined Spock, Coffin, and Goodman $5,000 each. Ferber, probably because he was a student, received a $1,000 fine.

In postdeliberation interviews with three of the jurors Mitford reports that:

> All three were strongly opposed to the Vietnam war, all expressed the highest regard for the defendants as individuals and for what they were trying to accomplish—and all said they felt, after hearing the judge's charge, that they had no alternative but to find them guilty. . .
>
> After talking with the jurors we were left with the impression that Raskin's acquittal stemmed not from any special merit that would distinguish his case from the others, but rather from a tacit desire of the jury to assert its independence, to vote, in some token way, its conscience.[33]

The defendants appealed their verdict to the Court of Appeals for the 1st Circuit, and the Appeals Court reversed. On August 8, 1969, the Justice Department said it would drop the matter. All the defendants were released.

Political Trials of the Mid-1970s

The last group of trials concern the Watergate Cover-Up. For this period, I review the Mitchell-Stans trial and the Cover-Up trial involving John Ehrlichman, H. Robert Haldeman, John Mitchell, Robert Mardian, and Kenneth Parkinson.

The defendants in these trials differ in important ways from any of the defendants considered hitherto with the possible exception of Alger Hiss. They were all prominent members of the government. Until their indictment, they represented the "establishment" at least of the executive branch of the federal government. Several of them (for example, Mitchell and Mardian) were directly responsible for the indictments of defendants in the political trials of the previous period. They exuded authority, connections, prestige, and wealth. How did such defendants fare at the hands of the jury?

On January 6, 1975, a jury in Washington, D.C., composed of nine women and three men, of eight blacks and four whites, deliberated for fifteen hours and found the defendants in the Watergate Cover-Up trial (John Mitchell, former attorney general, H.R. Haldeman, chief of staff to the president, John Ehrlichman, the president's chief of the Domestic Council, Robert Mardian, chief of the Internal Security Division of the Justice Department under Mitchell) guilty of conspiracy, perjury, and obstruction of justice. Kenneth Parkinson, a Washington attorney who worked for the 1972 Committee to Re-Elect the President, was acquitted.

Unlike the jury in the Rosenberg case, which was composed of eleven whites, one black, no Jews, and no laborers, the jurors selected to hear the Watergate trial seemed to represent a cross-section of Washington, D.C. society: a doorman, a clerk in a dime store, a retired maid, a clerical worker at George Washington University, a loan specialist for the Department of Agriculture. The foreman was a retired U.S. Parks police sergeant.

Judge John Sirica sentenced the four guilty defendants to from thirty months to eight years in prison. Their convictions were upheld by the Appellate Court.

Less than a year prior to the Watergate Cover-Up trial, another trial involving one of the defendants in the Watergate trial, John Mitchell, and another former member of the Nixon cabinet, Maurice Stans (secretary of commerce) took place in the U.S. District Court for the Southern District of New York. The major charge against the two defendants was conspiracy to impede a Securities and Exchange Commission investigation of Robert L. Vesco, a financier and a fugitive at the time of the trial, in return for a $200,000 cash contribution to President Nixon's reelection campaign.

Before the jury of nine men and three women was finally selected, 196 prospective jurors had been examined. The twelve selected included a bank teller, a steel cutter, a telephone installer, a Western Union messenger, a mail room supervisor, a post office supervisor, a city highway department employee, a shipping clerk foreman, a subway conductor, an insurance company clerk, and an elderly retired lady who became ill and was replaced by a vice-president of the First National City Bank.

The trial lasted ten weeks. The jury found the defendants not guilty. Zeisel and Diamond report that the jury on their first ballot were divided eight for conviction, four for acquittal.[34] Zeisel-Diamond examined the role played by one of the jurors and concluded as follows:

> This jury came as close to the film story in *Twelve Angry Men* as one is likely to see in real life. In the film, Henry Fonda, one of the jurors, succeeded in reversing a first ballot that stood 11 to 1 for conviction. It seems the Mitchell-Stans jury gained its Henry Fonda when, some weeks into the trial, juror Violet Humbert fell sick, and alternate Andrew Choa, a vice-president of the First National City Bank, took her place.
>
> . . .Choa's role in this trial fell into two parts: what he did while the trial was in progress and what he did during the deliberation. The one role, it will be seen, is connected to the other.
>
> During the many and long evenings, Choa had helped to break the monotony. Occasionally, he took his fellow jurors to the movies in the private auditorium of the bank. When the jurors asked to see the St. Patrick's Day parade and were told they could not go since this meant mingling with the street crowds, he arranged for them to watch it from one of the bank's branch offices. On one or more occasions when money was not readily available for minor jury expenses such as for entertainment, "Andrew paid, then the Government paid him back." Choa's bank also loaned baseball bats to the jury. He became, as the *New York Times* reporter put it, the jury's "social director." His fellow jurors could hardly help being obliged to the man who had used his high social position to make their sequestration more bearable.
>
> . . .We know that Choa was one of the four jurors who from the outset voted for acquittal and, one must presume, began the arduous task of converting the majority to his view. We know no details, but are told that he persuaded the jury at several points to have testimony as well as the judge's instructions reread. We do not know what testimony, but are told that these requests were drafted by Choa for the forelady's signature.
>
> When it came to the jury's appraisal of the memorandum written by Vesco (or an associate) to Nixon's brother, in which Vesco threatened to disclose his secret $200,000 cash contribution unless the SEC dropped his, Choa said he considered it "trash"—and the jury seemed to have agreed. The end is known. The unlikely event did happen; the eight jurors, who at one point thought the defendants guilty, changed their minds. Both defendants were acquitted on all counts.[35]

Perhaps it is because Zeisel is such a strong champion of the jury system, and perhaps because he believes that Mitchell and Stans in fact committed the acts for which they were charged, that he and Diamond place such emphasis on Choa's role. They show that initial jury voting splits of eight for guilty and four for not guilty will end up finding the defendant not guilty in only 5 percent of the cases. The 20 to 1 shot happened in the Mitchell-Stans trial. Zeisel and Diamond attribute that unusual result to an unusual juror—Andrew Choa. Their faith in the system is not shaken. Their belief, however, that protectors of the jury must always be vigilant is strengthened by the events in the Mitchell-Stans trial.

Concluding Remarks

In looking back on the jury's performance in the political trials of the 1950s, 1960s, and 1970s, we should note first that the defendants, the acts for which they were charged, and the ideology and political symbolism surrounding the trials differed considerably across the three time periods.

In the late 1940s and early 1950s international communism with the Soviet Union as its home base was perceived as the major threat to democracy in America. Public opinion and government officials were afraid that the United States would be subverted by its internal enemy—the Communist party and its multitudes of front groups and secret agents. The defendants on trial during the era were persons who were publicly associated with positions of leadership in the American Communist party (Dennis, Foster, and others) or persons whose membership in the party made them suspect, or persons who occupied responsible positions in government and were accused of belonging to communist cells and of being disloyal to the United States (Alger Hiss, Owen Latimore, William Remington all fall into this category). In almost all the political trials that were heard during this era the charges focused on the defendant's alleged disloyalty to the United States, his or her deception, and his or her identification with the Soviet Union. The socioeconomic and personal characteristics of the defendants varied considerably. Hiss, and his upper-middle class WASP background and mannerisms, was charged with the same type of traitorous acts as were Julius and Ethel Rosenberg who were part of the poor, Jewish intellectual-working class enclaves that lived on the lower east side of Manhattan.

The defendants, the issues, the charges, the political ideology, and symbolism of the late sixties differed markedly from the previous era of political trials. In the late sixties the defendants were young, many were well educated, some were black, practically all (Angela Davis was the major exception) disavowed any loyalty to the Soviet Union or to any foreign ideology. Their political activism grew out of their participation in student protests and demonstrations on college and university campuses or in the ghettoes of Oakland, Detroit, or Newark, where they experienced first hand the humiliation and discrimination that their black skin evoked.

The charges against the defendants in the late 1940s and early 1950s were those of disloyalty, spying, passing of secrets to enemy agents. But in the next era, political loyalty at least in the traditional sense of allegiance to one country as opposed to another was not an issue. Tom Hayden, Jerry Rubin, and Philip Berrigan were not accused of acting in the interests of a foreign government—

their actions, which included protests that erupted into violence, civil disobedience, burning of draft cards, inciting to rioting, had no foreign direction, support, or symbolism. So, too, did the motivations and identities of the Black Panthers originate wholly out of their American experience and lacked official foreign financial or moral endorsement.

Perhaps this absence of foreign interference and involvement is the single most important explanation for why the defendants in this era fared so much better at the hands of the jury than did the Rosenbergs, Dennis, Hiss, and others some twenty years earlier. All the defendants in the major political trials of the late 1940s and early 1950s were found guilty. All the convictions were upheld on appeal. Julius and Ethel Rosenberg were the first American citizens ever to be executed in peacetime for treason. None of the defendants who participated in the major political trials of the late 1950s were found guilty of the acts for which they were charged. Angela Davis and the thirteen defendants in the Panther trial in New York City were acquitted of all charges. The jury in the Harrisburg 7 trial hung ten in favor of acquittal, two for conviction and the government chose not to try them again. None of the defendants in the Chicago 8 trial was convicted of conspiracy to incite riot (the major charge), some were acquitted of all charges, the others were found guilty of the lesser charge of crossing state lines with intent to incite riot. Huey Newton was convicted of manslaughter, not first-degree murder, the act for which he was charged originally. In the Newton and Chicago 8 trials the decisions were reversed on appeal.

A few years later in the mid-1970s the jury found itself confronted with still another type of defendant and another set of charges. In the appearance of Maurice Stans and John Mitchell, the jury was asked to determine the guilt or innocence of two men who only a short while ago had been among the most respected and powerful people in the government. As members of the cabinet, as close personal friends and advisors to the president, as leaders of the Republican party, they had few peers to share the power and influence they exerted. The jury acquitted Stans and Mitchell.

H.R. Haldeman and John Ehrlichman had been portrayed in the press as assistant presidents, as men who themselves had no independent power, but who in their proximity to the president had access to the primary source of political power in the United States. For their participation in the planning, expediting, and cover-up of Watergate Mitchell, Haldeman, and Ehrlichman were found guilty and sentenced to from thirty months to eight years in prison.

During none of these periods is there any evidence, or indeed any suggestion, of the jury's lack of independence, or of the jury's failure to understand the issues or complexities of the problems involved, or of the jury's failure to do its duty. The lack of consistency speaks well for the jury—different issues, different defendants, different contexts, different evidence should and did make for different verdicts. In almost every trial, the jury deliberated for a long time. On the basis of post-trial interviews we gather they worked hard during the deliberations, reviewing the evidence, the instructions, and the arguments put forth by the defense and prosecuting attorneys. When the jury voted to acquit, in no instance did the government attack the integrity of its decision.

If one compares the consistent string of guilty verdicts reached by juries in the late 1940s and early 1950s and argues that the jury was reflecting popular support for political conformity and fear of deviant ideas, that the jury's verdict represented public concerns about loyalty rather than serving the rule of law—one would have to explain the string of not guilty verdicts reached by the same institution a decade-and-a-half later when popular opinion was just as favorable to political conformity and just as opposed and frightened by political dissent. The jury voted acquittal against blacks who threatened to blow the country up, against blacks and whites who openly ridiculed our society's most sacred symbols—its flag, its courts, its president.

The purpose of this chapter has not been to claim that the jury is beyond reproach or incapable of error. My aim has simply been to show how an institution run by amateurs, directed and organized by ordinary people, using their common sense, and following formal rules can perform its duty in a consistently responsible manner; how it can stand above popular prejudice and deliver verdicts that experts steeped and trained in the law respect.

Notes

1. Harry Kalven, Jr., and Hans Zeisel, *The American Jury,* (Boston: Little, Brown, 1966), pp. 6, 8, 18.
2. R. Simon, *Public Opinion in America: 1936--1970,* (Chicago: Rand McNally, 1975), pp. 5, 6.
3. Eugene Dennis (party secretary), Robert Thompson, Henry Winston, Gus Hall, John Williamson, Jack Stachel, Irving Potash, Carl Winter, Benjamin Davis, John Gates, and Gilbert Green were the 11 defendants. The trial of Party Chairman William Foster was postponed because of a serious heart condition.
4. "Doggonedest Trial," *Time,* April 11, 1949, p. 21.
5. "Dennis Trial," *Newsweek,* May 23, 1949.
6. Thompson, in recognition of his record during the war, was given a three-year sentence and a $10,000 fine.
7. The bar of the statute of limitations prevented indicting Hiss on the more serious offense.
8. R.B. Morris, *Fair Trial,* (New York: Harper and Row, 1967), p. 476.
9. David Greenglass was Ethel Rosenberg's brother.
10. *Supreme Court of the United States,* Transcript of Record, Vol. II, Book 4:1614, 1952.
11. The organizations that appeared on the attorney general's list included such ones as the School of Jewish Studies, the American Jewish Labor Council,

the Jewish Peoples' Committee. The Publications included the *National Guardian,* the *Daily Mirror,* and the *Journal American.*

12. R. Simon, "Public Opinion in America," p. 117.

13. The Pentagon Papers trial of Daniel Ellsberg and Anthony Russo, the Gainesville 8 trial, the Milwaukee 12 trial, are not included but are representative of the same genre. They are not discussed because of the exigencies of time and space.

14. S. Barkan, "Political Trials and the Pro Se Defendant in the Adversary System," *Social Problems* 24, no. 3 (1977) pp. 326, 328.

15. E. Kennebeck, *Juror Number Four* (New York: Norton, 1973), p. 338.

16. R. Major, *Justice in the Round* (New York: The Third Press, 1973), p. 283.

17. Ibid., p. 295.

18. Ibid., p. 300

19. Ibid., pp. 300, 301.

20. D. Danelski, "The Chicago Conspiracy Trial," in T.L. Becker (ed.), *Political Trials* (Indianapolis: Bobbs-Merrill, 1971), pp. 145, 151, 153, 176. Weiner was a native of Chicago who had received a B.A. from the University of Illinois and a master's degree in social work from Loyola University. Froines was born in Oakland, California, on June 13, 1939. After graduating from Berkeley in 1962, he spent a summer working in a black voter registration project in Louisiana and then went to Yale, where he received a Ph.D. in chemistry. While at Yale he joined Students for a Democratic Society (SDS) and worked in a black community project in New Haven. His SDS affiliation led to friendships with Davis and Hayden.

21. Ibid., p. 151.

22. Ibid., p. 153.

23. Ibid., p. 176. At first three of the jurors who had favored acquittal would not accept the compromise. They said the anti-riot law was unconstitutional. But that was not, a juror explained, for them to determine. They had only to decide if the defendants had violated the law.

24. Ibid., p. 176.

25. The seventh was a Muslim from Pakistan.

26. W. O'Rourke, The Harrisburg 7 and the New Catholic Left (New York: Thomas Y. Crowell, 1972), pp. 45, 71, 261.

27. Ibid, p. 71.

28. Ibid., p. 261.

29. At the end of the trial, Boyd Douglas, the man who shared a cell with Berrigan and who testified against him, was awaiting a decision by the FBI about how they would repay him for his services on the stand.

30. J. Mitford, *The Trial of Dr. Spock* (New York: Knopf, 1969), pp. 97, 98, 218, 219.

31. Ibid., p. 98.

32. Ibid., p. 218.

33. Ibid., p. 219.

34. In their article "The Jury Selection in the Mitchell-Stans Conspiracy Trial," *American Bar Foundation Research Journal,* vol. 1976, no. 1, Zeisel and Diamond report that the *New York Times* published an article by Martin Arnold based on interviews with some of the jurors. In that article he reported the 8–4 initial split.

35. H. Zeisel, and S. Diamond, "The Jury Selection in the Mitchell-Stans Conspiracy Trial," *American Bar Foundation Research Journal,* (1976):162.

Index

Index

Age
  jury selection and, 33
  representativeness of juries and, 30
Ahmad, Eqbal, 139
Alker, H.R., 30
American Bar Association Journal, 20
Apodaca v. *Oregon*, 73, 77
Arnason, Judge, 134
Atomic Energy Act of 1946, 129

Ballew v. *Georgia*, 75-76, 102
Barkan, S., 132
Barth, John, 12
Barton, A., 114-115
Benet, Stephen Vincent, 12, 14
Berelson, Bernard, 110
Berrigan, Philip, 139
Black, Justice, 129
Blacklists, 125
Black Panther Party, 132, 133, 136
Blacks, 133
  foreman selection and, 44
  magazine articles on, 18-19
  Panther 13 trial and, 132-133
  representativeness of juries and, 30
  verdicts and, 39
Branton, Leo, 133, 134
Brennan, Justice, 109
Broeder, Dale W., 38, 39, 45, 49, 57, 64
Burger, Chief Justice, 109

Challenges, 32
Chambers, Whittaker, 127-128
Change-of-venue motion, 117
Chase, Justice, 128
Chesterton, G.K., 18
Chicago 8 conspiracy trial, 126, 132, 135-138, 139
Chicago jury project, 3
  consensus studies in, 69
  jury selection and, 32, 36
  rationality of deliberations in, 52
  rules of law in, 53-54, 57
Choa, Andrew, 144
Christie, Richard, 36-37, 41
Civil rights movement, 18
Civil trials, 22, 50, 80
Civil War, 7
Clark, Ramsey, 138
Coffin, William Sloan, 132, 139-142
Colasanto, Diane, 52-53
Colgrove v. *Battin*, 73, 74, 75
Connally, John, 117
Connelly, Marc, 12, 14
Consensus, 63-69
Constitution, 6, 29
Continental Congress, 5
Cooper, James Fenimore, 12
Cornish, W.R., 39-40, 54-55

Damages, 57, 80
Danelski, D., 135-136, 137
Darrow, Clarence, 15, 33, 34
Davis, Angela, 117, 132, 133-135, 137
Davis, James H., 73-106
Decision rule, 77-78
  conceptual issues in, 79-85
  size of jury and, 78-79
Declaration of Independence, 6
Deliberations
  consensus in, 63-69
  expert testimony in, 57-63
  first ballot votes in, 64-65
  rationality of, 49-71
  rules of law and, 52-57
  similarity between judges' and juries, 50-52
Dellinger, David, 135
Democrats, 38
Dennis, Eugene, 125, 126-127, 130
Devlin, Lord, 22, 123
Diamond, S., 143-144
Dickey, William, 12
Dissent, political, 131
Doubt, reasonable, 55-57
Dreiser, Theodore, 12-13
Due process, 6

Duren v. *Missouri*, 31
Durham rule, 53, 54, 58

Educational factors, 30-31, 42, 43
Egan, Sister, 139
Ehrlichman, John, 142-143
Elkins, Stanley, 12
England, 5, 6
Espionage, 129
Ethnic factors, 34, 39
Experimental juries
  consensus studies in, 66-69
  decision rule and, 77-78
  expert testimony and, 58-60
  rationality of deliberations and, 52
  see also Chicago jury project
Expert testimony, 57-63

Faulkner, William, 12
Fay v. *New York*, 30
FBI, 136
Ferber, Michael, 139-142
Fiction, 11-14
Fifteenth Amendment, 7
First Amendment, 123
First ballot votes, 64-65
Ford, Francis J., 139-142
Foreman selection, 43-45
Fourteenth Amendment, 6, 7, 132-133
Frank, Jerome, 20-22
Fugitive Slave Law, 7

Garry, Charles, 31
Gates, John, 126
Gelfand, A.E., 100-101
Gignoux, Judge, 137
Goddard, Henry, 125
Goodman, Mitchell, 139-142
Greenglass, David, 129

Haldeman, H. Robert, 142-143
Hall, Gus, 126
Hand, August, 129
Hand, Learned, 30
Harrisburg 7 trial, 36-37, 138-139
Hawkins, Charles, 41, 44, 45, 66-67, 70
Hayden, Tom, 135, 136, 137
Hiss, Alger, 125, 127-129, 130
History of juries, 5-8
Hoffman, Julius, 126, 135, 136, 137, 139
House Un-American Activities Committee, 128
Hung juries, 63-64, 79

Incest trials, 39, 52, 58
Insanity defense
  expert testimony in, 57-63
  instructions of judges and, 61-63
  sex differences in verdicts with, 39
Instructions of judges
  expert testimony and, 58
  insanity plea and, 61-63
  pretrial publicity and, 111

Jamestown, Virginia, 5
Jews, 130, 133
Johnson, Bruce, 3
Johnson v. *Louisiana*, 73, 77
Joiner, Charles, 23-24
Judges, view of jury by, 20-25
Justice Department, 125-142

Kadish, Mortimer R., 7-8
Kadish, Sanford H., 7-8
Kalven, Harry, Jr., 3, 7, 19, 24, 38, 49, 51, 52, 65, 77
Kaplan, John, 118
Kaufman, George, 12, 14
Kaufman, Irving R., 125, 129-130, 142
Kessler, Joan B., 69, 70
King, Kristi, 136
Kissenger, Henry, 138
Klapper, Joseph, 110
Knebel, Fletcher, 19-20
Kunstler, William, 126, 132, 135, 136, 137

Lee, Harper, 12, 13
Lehman, Godfrey, 37
Life, 18-19
Literature, 11-14
Look, 19, 20
Loyalty programs and oaths, 124-125

McAlister, Elizabeth, 139
McCarran Internal Security Act, 125
McCarthy, Joseph, 125
McCleery, Ray Carl, 37
McLaughlin, Father, 139
M'Naghten rule, 54, 58
Magazines, 14-20
Major, R., 134-135
Majority rule, 77-78
Mann, Abbie, 135
Mann, Richard, 41
Mardian, Robert, 142-143
Marshall, Justice, 109
Marshall, Prentice, 5
Mass media
  image of jury in, 14-20
  pretrial publicity and, 109-121
  public attitudes, opinions, and, 110-111
Medical expert testimony, 57-61
Medina, Harold, 125, 126-127
Men
  foreman selection and, 44
  jury selection and, 33
  participation in decisions and, 41-42
  verdicts and, 39
Miller, Arthur, 12
Mitchell, John, 117, 142-145
Mitford, J., 140
Mundt-Nixon bill, 125
Muste, A.J., 135

Nebraska Press Association v. *Stuart*, 109-110, 111, 117, 118
Newspapers, 109-121
Newsweek, 20, 37, 127
Newton, Huey, 132-133
New York Times Magazine, 17-18
Nizer, Louis, 31-32
Novels, 11-14

Occupational factors, 34, 42-43
O'Dwyer, Paul, 138
O'Rourke, W., 139

Parkinson, Kenneth, 142-143
Perception, 110
Personal injury cases, 57
Personality characteristics, 34-35
Peterson, Ruth, 136
Political parties, 38
Political trials
  late 1940s and early 1950s, 124-130
  late 1960s and early 1970s, 131-142
  mid-1970s, 142-145
Pound, Roscoe, 7
Pretrial publicity, 109-121
Probabilities in verdicts, 82-91
Proof, burden of, 55
Public opinion
  on dissent, 131
  loyalty oaths during McCarthy period and, 125
  mass media influence on, 110-111
  pretrial survey of, 115-117
Publicity, pretrial, 109-121
Psychiatry, 59-61
Psychoanalytic literature, 110-111
Psychologists, 36

Racial factors
  foreman selection and, 44
  magazine articles on, 18-19
  representativeness of juries and, 30
Rand, Ayn, 12, 14
Rap Brown Law, 135
Rape trials, 39
Raskin, Marcus, 139-142
Rationality of juries, 49-71
Reader's Digest, 15-16, 19, 20
Reasonable doubt principle, 55-57
Religious factors, 34
Representativeness of juries, 29-31
  Panther 13 trial and, 132-133
  Rosenberg case and, 130, 133
Republicans, 38
Rice, Elmer, 12, 14
Rifkind, Simon, 23
Right of trial, 6
Riley, John and Matilda, 110
Riordin, Dennis, 31
Robeson, Paul, 125
Role playing, 4

Rosenberg, Ethel and Julius, 127, 129-130, 133, 142
Rubin, Jerry, 135
Rules of Law, 52-57

Sacher, Harry, 126
Sanders, Joseph, 52-53
Saturday Evening Post, 16-17
Schulman, Jay, 36, 37, 41, 138
Seale, Bobby, 135, 136, 137
Sealy, A.P., 39-40, 54-55
Selection of jurors, 31-38
 age and sex in, 33
 personality factors in, 34-35
 religious and ethnic background in, 34
 socioeconomic characteristics, in, 33-34
Selective Service Act, 139
Self-esteem, 110
Sex differences
 foreman selection and, 44
 jury selection and, 33
 participation in decisions and, 41-42, 43
 verdicts and, 39
Simon, Caroline K., 17
Simon, Rita, J., 49, 57
Sirica, John, 143
Sixth Amendment, 6
Size of jury, 73-106
 conceptual issues, in, 79-85
 decision rule and, 78-79
 empirical research concerning, 73-77
 models for, 100-101
 probabilities and, 86-91
 social decision rules and, 91-98
 social-decision-scheme matrices for, 82-85
 speed of verdict and, 76
 Supreme Court decisions on, 74-76, 88
 thought experiments in, 85-86
 verdict possibilities and, 80-82
Slavery, 7
Smith Act, 125, 127
Smith v. *Texas*, 29
Sobell, Morton, 129
Social decision rules, 82-85, 91-98
Social factors, and verdicts, 38-41
Social scientists, 36, 41, 138
Socioeconomic factors
 jury selection and, 33-34
 verdicts and, 39-40
Solomon, H., 100-101
Southern states, 7
Speed of verdict, 76
Spock, Benjamin, 132, 139-142
Stanford Law Review, 118
Stans, Maurice, 142, 143-145
State Department, 125
Stephan, Cookie, 38, 39
Stevens, Justice, 109
Stewart, Justice, 109
Strodtbeck, Fred L., 41, 49, 57
Supreme Court
 due process and, 6
 jury size and, 73, 74, 75-76, 88
 pretrial publicity and, 109-110, 117
 representativeness of juries and, 29-30, 31
 Rosenberg case and, 129
Swain v. *Alabama*, 30
Swan, Justice, 129

Taylor v. *Louisiana*, 31
Testimony, expert, 57-63
Theater, 11-14
Thiel v. *Southern Pacific Co.*, 30
Thirteenth Amendment, 7
Thought experiments, 85-86, 99, 100
Time, 20
Tocqueville, Alex de, 6-7

Un-American Activities Committee (House), 128
United States v. *Dennis*, 30
 U.S. News and World Report, 3
University of California Board of Regents, 125

Verdicts
 Similarities between juries' and judges', 50-52
 see also Instructions of judges

Vesco, Robert L., 143
Virginia Company, 5
Voir dire
  function of, 32
  Harrisburg 7 trial and, 138
  pretrial publicity and, 110-111,
    114-115
  Rosenberg case and, 130
Vollrath, David A., 73-106

Warren, Robert Penn, 12, 13-14
Watergate Cover-Up, 142-145
Watts, Emily S., 12, 14
Wenderoth, Father, 139
White, Justice, 109
Williams v. *Florida*, 73, 74, 75, 88
Winston, Henry, 126
Women
  foremen selection and, 44
  jury selection and, 33
  participation in decisions by, 41-42
  representativeness of juries and bias
    against, 30-31
  verdicts and, 39

Yale Social Psychology Laboratory,
  110
Zeisel, Hans, 3, 7, 19, 24, 38, 49, 51,
  52, 64, 65, 74, 77, 143-144
Zenger, John Peter, 5

About the Author

Rita J. Simon is professor of sociology, communications research, and law, and director of the Graduate College Program in Law and Society at the University of Illinois. She is editor of *The American Sociological Review* and is author or editor of the following books and monographs: *The Jury and the Defense of Insanity; As We Saw the Thirties; Readings in the Sociology of Law; Payment for Pain and Suffering* (with Jeffrey O'Connell); *American Public Opinion: 1937–1970; Women and Crime; The Jury System in America; Transracial Adoption* (with Howard Altstein); *Continuity and Change: A Study of Two Ethnic Communities in Israel; Research in Law and Sociology; The Criminology of Deviant Women* (with Freda Adler). Professor Simon has contributed numerous articles to professional journals.